Rise of Christianity in Arunachal Pradesh

Rise of Christianity in Arunachal Pradesh

JAMES WANGLAT

Copyrights © 2020 James Wanglat

All rights reserved. No part of this book may be reproduced, stored, or transmitted by any means-whether auditory, graphical, mechanical, or electronic-without written permission of the author. Any unauthorized reproduction of any part of this book is illegal and is punishable by law.

To the maximum extent permitted by law, the author and publisher disclaim all responsibility and liability to any person, arising directly or indirectly from any person taking or not taking action based on the information available in this publication.

ISBN 13: 978-93-90025-09-1
ISBN 10: 93-90025-09-5

Printed in India and published by BUUKS.

Dedicated to my mother Senphiak who understood the difficulties but asked for strength, grace, love and forgiveness to get through the passage of time.

Life's sorrows never left her until she found her Redeemer. She served Him and the Church without seeking any title.

"We must embrace pain and burn it as fuel for our journey."

– Kenji Miyazawa

ACKNOWLEDGEMENTS

Fr. P. K. George and the Catholic Association of Tirap were instrumental in encouraging me to research and catalogue all the journals, notings and documents collected by me over the years about the events that unfolded in the state of Arunachal Pradesh in a more tangible form.

Most of these documents were scattered in three places, in my Borduria village home, in my office in Itanagar and in my house in Shillong. I finally brought everything together in one place and segregated them in 26 voluminous files. Then began the herculean task of sorting out the documentation on the various instances of persecution. Initially, Lanwang Sumpa, Manwang Loho and Ms Mattey spent many hours transcribing the documents into my office computer. I sorted through the transcriptions and prepared a sketchy manuscript. The information ran to more than 2000 pages initially.

After reducing it further to about 800 pages, the raw descriptive manuscript was shared with Tarun Kumar Sarkar, my childhood friend from our days in Mount Hermon School, Darjeeling. He burnt the midnight oil to whittle the manuscript down to around 500 pages. Thereafter, both of us sat, brainstormed and argued over a period of six months to edit the manuscript and to give it its final shape for publication. I could never have done it without Tarun's help and advice.

It has truly been a labour of love and dedication and a culmination of years of research, collation of data and information to bring to the readers an authentic and well-documented account of the persecution of Christians in Arunachal Pradesh.

CONTENTS

Preface		xiii
1	Introduction	1
2	The Land of the Rising Sun	6
3	Growth of Christianity in Arunachal Pradesh	12
4	Religious Policy of the Administration and its Implementation	18
5	Chronicle of Persecution	26
6	Consecration of the First Catholic Church in Arunachal Pradesh	38
7	Conclusion	59

Annexure — 63

1. Important Christian Leaders of Arunachal Pradesh — 65
2. Borduria Church Builders — 69
3. Baptism of Catholics—Important Dates — 73
4. Christian Chronicles of Arunachal Pradesh in Brief — 75
5. Articles on Persecution of Christians in Arunachal Pradesh — 82
   Kutcha Church — 83
   Sentiments of the Tribal People — 84
   Tribals Who Reconverted to Their Original Faiths — 85
   Demolition of Churches — 86
   Destruction of Christian Homes — 87
   Story Behind the Demolition — 88

	The Untold Tale of Arunachal Pradesh	90
	Weeding Out Christianity	90
	What the Christians Ask For	92
	Did Christian Missionaries Detribalize the North-East?	93
	Christians Are Accused of Bringing in "Westernization"	95
	What the Missionary Has Really Done	101
	Do Figures Show an "Alarming Rate of Growth" of Christians?	104
	Is Isolation the Solution?	106
	A Philosophy for NEFA by Elwin— A Liability or an Asset?	107
	Freedom to Choose	111
	The Unsecular Face of Secular India	112
	Is Hinduisation a Solution?	113
	The Tragedy of Arunachal Pradesh (NEFA)	115
	The Underground Church	118
6	An Unwise Bill—Freedom of Religion Bill	125
7	Arunachal Pradesh Freedom of Religion Act, 1978, and Related Documents	129
8	Universal Declaration of Human Rights—Article 18	139
	Documents Related to the Persecution of Christians	141

PREFACE

My goal in writing this book is twofold.

First, I wish to recount how I worked to coordinate the efforts of the representatives of various Christian denominations in Arunachal Pradesh to stand up and protest unitedly against the persecution of Christians. The different Christian organizations of Northeast India decided to constitute a committee known as the Arunachal Christian Action Committee (ACAC), and I was elected as the Chairman (which I served for ten years consecutively).

Second, I write to give readers a perspective on how the outstanding Constitution of India can be violated with impunity to serve the thinkers of North and South Blocks of Raisina Hill, New Delhi. From the late seventies to the nineties, the anti-Christian philosophy of the NEFA administration was implemented by the officials and elected representatives of the state government with extra vigor. Many of the decisions taken by the NEFA administration were devoid of any vision for growth and development of the area. Instead, Christianity was targeted and portrayed as a foreign religion instigated by the CIA and Western countries. This was mischievous and unethical.

In the pages that follow, I have done my best to write about the persecution of Christians in Arunachal Pradesh as I saw it and about the growth of Christianity in the state surmounting all obstacles and the devious strategies of the administration. If circumstances gave me a chance to do things differently, I certainly would not. I would not hesitate to write about what I saw in my forty-four years of public service as Chairman of ACAC and as an elected MLA. One has to do what one believes is right and accept the consequences. Serving the people was an honor of a lifetime, and I appreciate being given an opportunity to share the story of persecution of Christians in Arunachal Pradesh. My hope is that this book will serve as a resource for anyone studying this period in the history of the state.

The narrative on persecution of Christians in Arunachal Pradesh is based primarily on my recollections. I believe it will be impossible to reach definitive conclusions on how and when persecution against Christians started. Passage of time allows passions to cool, results to clarify, and scholars to compare different approaches to persecution of Christians in the state. With help from researchers, I have authenticated my account with government documents; personal notes; articles written during that time; interviews with Father M. C. Thomas, SDB, and other individuals and groups; news reports; and also with inputs from Toko Kach's book Growth of Baptist Churches and Impact on Socio-Culture Life of the Nyishi Tribe in Arunachal Pradesh, the Upper Subansiri Baptist Churches Association, and other sources. If there are inaccuracies in this book, the responsibility is mine.

The rate of growth of Christianity in Arunachal Pradesh was the fastest when persecution of Christians was at its peak. Throughout the book, I have tried to describe how the good intentions of Nehruvian philosophy were cleverly misused to serve the whims and fancies of some twisted administrators of Arunachal Pradesh. The ACAC took the decision to register our protest against the persecution without confronting the administration in any way or going into any kind of litigation. It was a totally nonviolent movement focusing on expressing the will and thoughts of the Arunachalee with the intention to win the hearts of the persecutors and make them realize their mistakes. This approach has been vindicated with the resultant rise of Christianity.

I hope the book will also give you a better sense of why I made the decision to convert to the Christian faith after the Arunachal Pradesh Freedom of Religion Act 1978 was enacted although I was happy and comfortable with the Hindu Vaishnavite religion of my forefathers. Perhaps the book will also be useful for you to make your own choices in your life.

1

INTRODUCTION

Steve Jobs said, "Your time is limited. So don't waste it running someone else's life. Don't be trapped by dogma, which is living with other peoples' thinking. Don't let the noise of others' opinions drown out your inner voice. And most important have the courage to follow your heart and intuition."

And here I am telling you what I should have done a long, long time ago. This is the true story about the rise of Christianity in Arunachal Pradesh from less than 1 percent of the population in 1961 to more than 30 percent in 2011 as per the census data for the state. The figure is currently estimated to be between 50 and 60 percent.

I have been postponing the publication of this book for many years, wondering how my foes-turned-friends would react and what they would say. My inner voice tells me not to be drawn to the noise and opinion of what other people would feel! My intuition tells me to publish the book and, as Stewart Brand said, to "stay hungry and foolish."

If I did not share with future generations about what I saw, heard, and felt in the 1970s–1990s about the persecution of

Christians in independent India and, more specifically, in the land of the rising sun, NEFA (now called Arunachal Pradesh), then I would be committing a grave injustice to our people who fought a brave fight and suffered silently for their religious beliefs.

The events that unfolded in the cultural dynamics of Arunachal Pradesh in general, and erstwhile Tirap district in particular, are amazing. I am therefore speaking out for the thousands of unsung heroes who walked the path of epoch-making destiny in NEFA, and I have to tell you about their quest for religious freedom in free "Bharat" in the face of persecution by the administration.

Sadly, many of the leaders are no more. Steve Jobs rightly said, "Death is very likely the single best invention of life." He called it the life-changing agent. It clears out the old to make way for the new. I believe that the new generation should know about the old and how they suffered for their tomorrow.

Those of you from the current generation need to know the true story of what happened in the 1970s to the helpless "indigenous aborigines" of NEFA. Not very long from now, "you too will become old and be weeded away as many have been before" (Steve Job). And the thinking people of Arunachal Pradesh will understand why we should not persecute those who are different from us.

I will be naming some officials of the NEFA administration and politicians who directly or indirectly persecuted indigenous Arunachalee for accepting Christ. They had at that time embarked on a mission to stop the Christian church from coming to Arunachal Pradesh. Ironically this persecution, in fact, helped in the spreading of Christianity in Arunachal Pradesh.

Before I write more about persecution of Christians in Arunachal Pradesh, I ask for their forgiveness, just as I have long forgiven them for the pain and the suffering they inflicted on thousands of the faithful during the 1970s when the forbidden land was hidden behind a bamboo curtain, similar to the iron curtain in the USSR. Many of such persecutors have now accepted Jesus as their personal savior. And some of them have become pastors and builders of Christian churches in the state.

In Robin Sharma's perception, "In forgiveness we can all be free from the ugly past. It will bring peace and contentment and help us to enjoy life." If we do not forgive each other, we will be prisoners of our emotions. We have all sinned against God. But God's love for us is greater than our sin against him. And our forgiveness was made possible through the death of Christ on the cross in Calvary. We are no longer enemies but children of God. Let us forgive each other so that all of us can enjoy the beauty and mystery of life.

Robin Sharma says, "When you bear a grudge against someone, it is almost as if you carry that person around on your back with you. He drains you of your energy, enthusiasm and peace of mind. But the moment you forgive him, you let him off your back and you can move on with the rest of your life." Mark Twain too wrote, "Forgiveness is the fragrance that the violet sheds on the heel that crushed it."

The following persons, at some point of time in their lives, were very much against Christianity. Some were in the beginning overzealously anti-Christian, others were nominally so:

- P. K. Thungon, former chief minister of Arunachal Pradesh who introduced the Arunachal Pradesh Freedom of Religion Act 1978
- Gegong Apang, former chief minister of Arunachal Pradesh for twenty-three years

- T. L. Rajkumar, former speaker and minister for twenty-five years
- Most Ministers and MLAs from the late 1970s till the mid-1990s
- Wanglin Lowangdong, the chief of Borduria and former minister (later converted to Christianity and has been instrumental in establishing the growing Baptist Church in Tirap District. I supported him in allocating Borduria village land at Poakom for the establishment of the Tirap Baptist Mission/Council)
- Late Tadar Tang, former minister
- Nabum Atum, former Chairman of Arunachal Pradesh Civil Service
- Nabum Rebia, former chief secretary of All Subansiri Students' Union, former MP, speaker and minister
- Late Takar Tachi, former minister
- Late Ita Pulo, former MLA (later converted to Christianity and donated a building and land to the Catholic Church in Roing of Dibang Valley District)
- Wangkap Lowang retired Political Assistant (later converted to Christianity and became Deacon of Pansumthong Baptist Church. At 108 years of age, he is very active in his faith and spreading of the Gospel to the unreached.)
- Late Chewang Chena, Political Interpreter (later joined the Baptist Church, the very church he persecuted)
- Late Chowrong Longphi, Political Interpreter (later joined the TBCC Baptist Church)
- Late Kemsang Kenglang, Social Organizer
- Jagir Singh, SSB Area Organiser who was given out-of-turn promotions and retired as Secretary to the Government of Arunachal Pradesh

- B. Kumar, EAC, Sagalee
- Most of the political officers and the district administration

The government of Arunachal Pradesh and the political leadership tried to circumvent the constitution of our great country by enacting a draconian law called the "Arunachal Pradesh Freedom of Religion Act 1978." Col. K. A. A. Raja, Lieutenant Governor of Arunachal Pradesh, and P. K. Thungon, the first chief minister of the state, were the main persons responsible for its enactment. The intention was to stop any person from converting to Christianity in particular, even if he or she did so voluntarily, and to prevent any Christian missionary from entering the state. To the administration, all Christians were persona non grata.

Little did they imagine or comprehend that the laity would be the foundation of the Catholic Church in Arunachal Pradesh long before priests or preachers were allowed to enter the state (a fact now conveniently forgotten by priests from outside the state, namely from Kerala, Bihar, and Assam). The simple local indigenous people were the pillars and builders of churches in Arunachal Pradesh and were instrumental in making the faith accessible to those who needed them. It is because of them that the Church grew in Arunachal Pradesh with the Gospel spreading like wildfire.

It must also be understood that the majority of the tribals and indigenous people embraced Christianity on their own free will and not as a result of any force, inducement or deceitful means, or through illegal conversion. I cannot vouch for everyone though. It is quite possible that some of them might have converted to the Christian faith hoping to get admission for their wards in good Christian educational institutions, but, for most, it was by choice.

2

THE LAND OF THE RISING SUN

A Brief History

The state of Arunachal Pradesh, situated in the extreme northeast of the country, is, by area, the largest state of the Northeast region of India. It shares international boundaries with Bhutan, China (Tibet), and Myanmar to the west, north, and east, respectively, and state boundaries with Assam and Nagaland to the south and southeast.

Nature has endowed the state with amazing geographical and biological diversity. Most of the state is hilly, with difficult terrain, deep gorges, rivers, and streams, and there is perennial snow in the upper reaches. The hills have acted as natural boundaries for the different tribes and communities that inhabit the state and insulated them from each other as well as from the influences of the rest of the country. The terrain consists of mountain ranges toward the north and the east of the state sloping down to the plains of Assam, divided into valleys by the rivers Siang, Kameng, Subansiri, Dibang, Lohit, Dihing, and Tirap, which all flow into the Brahmaputra to the south.

The area is believed to have been inhabited since prehistoric times, but there is no written history of the area. All that is known is through oral traditions. People from Bhutan, Tibet, Burma (Myanmar), Yunnan Province of China, and Siam (Thailand) migrated over the centuries and settled down in the state. These tribal clans were isolated and insulated from each other because of the topography and developed their own languages, dialects, and cultural traditions. The state was never ruled directly either by the Ahoms or by neighboring countries or later by the British. The Ahoms, however, maintained contact with the tribes in the south mainly for trade and barter.

The modern history of Arunachal Pradesh began with the inception of British rule in Assam after the Anglo-Burmese war, which ended with the peace treaty negotiated with Burma on February 24, 1826. Thereafter, the British exercised their control over the Brahmaputra valley and made it a part of Bengal. However, like the Ahoms, they too followed a policy of isolating the hill tribes from the people of the plains.

In 1873, Assam was separated from Bengal and became its own province. The hill areas adjoining the plains districts were designated as non-regulated territory loosely administered by deputy commissioners of adjoining plains districts and kept out of the purview of the laws of the country. They were separated by the "Inner Line," a boundary along the foothills and prescribed under the Bengal Eastern Frontier Regulation 1873, which was introduced to protect British interests and for regulating the entry of non-hills people into the area. This resulted in very limited interaction between the hill areas and the rest of the country, and the people continued to live as before preserving their identity, culture, and way of life.

In 1914, some tribal areas of Assam were separated from the then Darrang and Lakhimpur districts of Assam to form the

North-East Frontier Tract. At the time of independence in 1947, the present territory of Arunachal Pradesh was considered as a tribal area of Assam. The territory was renamed as North-East Frontier Agency in 1954. NEFA was scheduled as an "Excluded Area" of Assam between 1950 and 1965 and administered by the Governor of Assam as an agent of the President of India. Because of its strategic importance, however, it was under control of the Ministry of External Affairs until 1965 and subsequently of the Ministry of Home Affairs. In 1972, NEFA was constituted as a Union Territory and renamed Arunachal Pradesh. On February 20, 1987, it became the twenty-fourth state of the Indian Union.

The name Arunachal Pradesh is very apt and beautiful. It is a Sanskrit name meaning the "Land of Dawn-lit Mountains" (or the Land of the Rising Sun) as the state receives the first rays of the sun, being situated in the north-easternmost extremity of the country. However, before renaming the newly born union territory, the Government of India and the administrators of NEFA should have consulted the cross section of the indigenous people, the headmen, and village authorities empowered under the Frontier Administration of Justice Regulation 1945, student unions, and others for their views before taking a decision on an appropriate name.

The People

Most of the states in the country were formed on linguistic lines but Arunachal Pradesh was not. It is an ethnic state inhabited by tribal people of diverse cultures and lifestyles, who form over 80 percent of the population. There are twenty-six major tribes and about 110 sub-tribes and minor tribes in the state. For hundreds of years, the mountains and river valleys have kept the various tribes isolated from each other and from the rest of the country. Each group has thus maintained its own distinct language, belief systems, culture, traditions, ways of life, myths, dialects, costumes, and dance and art forms.

The area has received migrations from different directions over centuries. There were migrations from Bhutan, Tibet, China, Burma (Myanmar), and Siam (Thailand) as well as from Assam and Nagaland where tribes with similar cultures still live. This is reflected in the linguistic heterogeneity of Arunachal Pradesh with as many as forty-six languages being spoken there. All the languages belong to the Tibeto-Chinese family with some belonging to the Siamese-Chinese and Tibeto-Burman sub groups. As a result, the tribes of Arunachal Pradesh have more in common and are more akin to the people of Bhutan, Tibet, Yunnan, and Burma than those of the Indian subcontinent. Arunachal Pradesh is culturally at least as much part of Southeast Asia as it is of South Asia.

Every tribe had a village council. These councils solved issues pertaining to kinship and group activities and set moral standards and necessary regulations. The aborigines of NEFA also had customary laws and a time-tested dispute resolution mechanism. The disputes in tribal societies were resolved with the aid of the Frontier Administration of Justice Regulation 1945 along with the different customary laws of the aborigine tribes, each different from the other tribe in practice and belief. Most village councils also solved basic civil and criminal cases and played an important role in development activities. It is interesting to note that there was no police force in Arunachal Pradesh up until 1972, when it became a Union Territory, and the councils were responsible for maintaining peace and order.

With the administration being highly localized within a village or group of villages, there was very little communication with the representatives of the Government of India. Initially, the administrative headquarters manned by the Indian Frontier

Administrative Service was situated outside NEFA. For example, the Tirap Frontier Tract headquarter was in Margherita, now part of Assam, and so were Sadiya, Balipara, and Lakhimpur Frontier Tracts. There was thus very little interaction between the hill tribes of NEFA and the rest of India.

Religious Groupings

There are several major socio-religious groupings in Arunachal Pradesh: animists of the Tani family, animist Idu Mishmi followers of Nani Intaya, animists influenced by Hinduism, Vaishnavaite Hindus, Buddhists of the Mahayana and Hinayana Sects, and Christians.

Tanis consider themselves to be the descendants of Abo Tani, the primeval common ancestor or the first human being. They reside in the central districts of Arunachal Pradesh and foothills bordering Assam. The Apatani, Adi, Miri Tagin, Galo, and Nyishi tribes of Arunachal Pradesh believe in the worship of the sun and the moon—Donyi Polo.

Idu Mishmis are located in the Upper and Lower Dibang Valley districts and are believers in the Goddess Nani Intaya.

A number of smaller tribes also adhere to the animist religion that has been influenced by Hinduism. They inhabit Tirap, Changlang, Lohit, and Upper Dibang Valley Districts. The tribes that follow this religion are the Noctes, Wanchos, Tangsas, and various Mishmi groups. Unlike the Tanis, they do not emphasize on the sun and moon in their religious practices, nor the work of the spirits. Instead, they are believers of a number of gods and goddesses who are involved in their daily lives.

The Noctes, Wancho, Tangsa, Aka, and Miji came under the influence of Hinduism through the Vaishnavite movement of Assam. Lotha Khunbao, king of the Noctes, was a Theravada Buddhist when he migrated from the Yunnan Province of China through the Hukong Valley of Myanmar. He subsequently adopted Vaishnavism of the Bareghar Satra and became a disciple of Ram Atta of Merbil, Sasoni, Assam.

The Lamaistic tradition of Mahayana Buddhism is practiced by the Monpas and Sherdukpens who inhabit Tawang and West Kameng Districts and by the Memba and Khamba tribes along the border to the north. Buddhists of erstwhile Kameng district were part of Tibet owing allegiance to His Holiness, the Dalai Lama of Tibet.

Khamptis of Lohit District and the Singphos in Changlang District belong to the Hinayana (Theravada) Sect of Buddhism, which they brought with them when they migrated from Burma and Siam.

Christianity made its beginnings in NEFA in the nineteenth century with the establishment of the Baptist Mission at Sadiya and was followed by the Roman Catholic priests from the Society of Paris Foreign Missions, namely Fr. Nicholas-Michel Krick and Fr. Augustin-Etienne Bourry who entered the "Abor Country" (a name given by British writers) in 1851. In 1854, they decided to expand their mission of evangelization to Tibet. On their journey to Tibet through NEFA in 1857, they were captured and killed by the Mishmi tribe in the village of Somme, which is near Kibato of Lohit District. (Kibato receives the first rays of the sun in India.) However, there is neither any written history of their mission nor of their work in NEFA.

3

GROWTH OF CHRISTIANITY IN ARUNACHAL PRADESH

According to the Arunachal Baptist Church Council, the history of Christianity in Arunachal Pradesh can be traced back to as early as the arrival of Mrs. C. A. Bruce in 1834 and Rev. Nathan Brown, the first American Baptist Missionary, in Sadiya, Assam. Their first task was to establish schools for the people of the foothills and for tribals in "Abor Country" or the Adi of Siang District.

The first missionary to reach the Naga Hills is believed to be one Rev. Miles Bronson, an American Baptist pastor who made his first journey to Namsang in 1839, where he opened a mission among the Nocte Nagas. Bronson was discouraged because of the lack of interest shown on the part of the local people (the Namsamgia were practicing Vaishnavite Hindus) and withdrew to Jaipur in Assam.

The Baptists had not totally abandoned the Arunachalee and began to make contact with them from their mission in Sadiya. The Baptist Church translated the New Testament into dialects like the Abor (now Adi) and Nyishi and made inroads in converting the indigenous NEFA tribals to Christianity.

Today, there are numerous Christian denominations in the state due to internal conflicts that caused the communities to split into smaller Protestant Churches. The Christian Revival Church is growing by leaps and bounds. Former Deputy Chief Minister Kameng Dollo joined this congregation with many of his supporters and so did other former Ministers and MLAs as well as retired IAS and IPS officers. The CRC constructed the first air-conditioned church in the state of Arunachal Pradesh at Itanagar.

Today the Catholic Church is the largest group among different Christian denominations in Arunachal Pradesh. Their active mission work, however, started only after 1979. The Catholic Church had two visionary Salesian priests, namely Bishop Robert Kerketta, SDB, and Fr. Thomas Menamparampil, SDB, who subsequently was elevated to Archbishop. From 1975 to 1981, Fr. Thomas was the Rector of Don Bosco Technical School in Shillong. On June 19, 1981, he was appointed by Pope John Paul II as bishop of the Diocese of Dibrugarh (East Arunachal was then a part of the Dibrugarh Diocese) and was elevated to Archbishop on July 10, 1995. Fr. Thomas is the author of over 180 articles on various subjects on evangelism, culture, ministry, education, religious life, and prayer. Fr. Thomas acted as the mediator in the conflict between the various ethnic groups in the State of Assam. He was nominated for the Noble Peace Price in 2011, and his nomination recognized his continued commitment to have peace, reconciliation, and stability in Northeast India, an area full of territorial and ethnic conflicts.

Fr. Thomas adopted laity evangelization and started with lay missionaries from different tribes of Arunachal Pradesh with the help of Bishop Kerketta of Dibrugarh Diocese and Bishop

Mithatani of Tezpur Diocese. The mission was to encourage the laity to preach the Gospel, weaving it with local cultural themes, and adopted, just as the Catholic Church did in Africa, ritual practices into the way of worship. As a result of such lucid vision and strategies, many hardcore anti-Christian leaders were convinced to join the Catholic Church, in particular, and Christian Churches in general. It is very interesting to note that the different Christian Churches in Arunachal Pradesh are not rigid in their doctrine in accepting nonbelievers into the Christian faith and abstain from excommunicating its members if they are involved in extramarital affairs or if they decide to take more than one wife.

Pope John Paul II, in his message for the World Congress of Ecclesial Movements and New Communities, emphasized the essential role of the layperson in the church's mission. He said: "There is so much need today for mature Christian personalities, conscious of their baptismal identity, of their vocation and mission in the Church and in the world!" The actual teaching of the church is that laypeople have a distinct and very real role in the spreading of the Gospel. In its mission, the work of the laity is the crucial means by which the world is to encounter Christ. Pope Francis has also powerfully expressed the importance of the laity in his address to the Laity Council: "We are in need of well-formed laypeople, animated by a pure and fresh faith, whose life has been touched by a personal and merciful encounter with the love of Jesus Christ. We are in need of laypeople who risk, who soil their hands, who are not afraid of erring, who go forward. We are in need of laypeople with vision of the future, not closed in the little things of life. And I have said it to young people: we are in need of laypeople with the taste of experience of life, who dare to dream."

Late Bishop Kerketta and Fr. Menamparampil introduced the following highly motivated and dedicated youth to the Catholic

Church and used them to spread the Gospel to those who had not heard about Jesus: Late Ranlam Dada of Borduria village, Tero Kakho of Kaimai Village (the first official Catechist of Arunachal Pradesh), Late Matwang Chimyang of Lapnan village, Anok Wangsa (former Minister) of Pongchow village (who joined the Baptist Church in the early nineties), Late Wintum Sawin of Lanwang Village, Pongbo Wangsa of Longphong village, Late Pulai of Longphong village, Chakpha Wangsu of Chatong village, Mossang of Nampong village, Somlung Mossang of Miao, Changlang District, Late Tadar Tanyang (former minister) of the then Subansiri District (now Kurung Kumey), Boa Tamo (former MLA) of Raga, Late Lokan Tado (former MLA) of Palin, Takam Sanjoy (former Minister and MP) of Palin, Late Madan Laling of Ziro, Late Gyati Taka of Ziro, and many other unsung heroes and apostles of the Catholic Church.

Most of them were students of Don Bosco Schools in Shillong, Dibrugarh, Jorhat, Dimapur, and Harmuti and of Lakhimpur Catholic Mission. When these students returned for their school vacations and holidays, the tribes began to notice a transformation in them. These young people opened their minds to new ideas and ways of thinking and living. They advocated self respect, freedom from oppression, dignity, and, above all, the love of Christ. The tribes responded with increasing eagerness to the influence of the education offered in the Salesian schools. More and more students went to Christian mission schools, and many Salesian alumni today hold important positions in both political and administrative offices of governance in the state of Arunachal Pradesh.

In 1992, the Salesian congregation decided to open Don Bosco School at Tinsukia with Fr. P. K. George, SDB, heading the institution while Fr. C. C. Jose was given the charge of

Harmuti Bosco School as the Rector of the institution. These institutions in Assam catered to the need for education of the students of Arunachal Pradesh. Christian institutions were not allowed to work inside the state till 1999. There was a complete ban on the entry of Christian priests and pastors to work with the villagers of Arunachal Pradesh, thanks to the rigid and anti-Christian policies unleashed by the P. K. Thungon and Gegong Apang governments. In spite of that, the Christian population grew from strength to strength.

From 1990, a few of us worked overtime, meeting various officials of North and South Blocks, Raisina Hill, New Delhi, for the creation of Catholic Dioceses in Arunachal Pradesh. My basic argument in support of the creation of dioceses in the state was that by creating Catholic Church Dioceses, the Government of India would go one step further in consolidating our country's rightful claim over Arunachal Pradesh being an integral part of India against China's perpetual claim over the territory. The word "China" did the magic trick even with the die-hard Hindu bureaucrats who were working overtime to ensure that Arunachal became a 100 percent Hindu state.

As a result of our efforts, the Holy See granted Arunachal Pradesh two Dioceses with the creation of the Miao Diocese and the Itanagar Diocese in December 2005. Bishop George Palliparambil's Episcopal Ordination took place in Miao on February 26, 2006, while the first bishop of Itanagar, Reverend John Thomas Kattrukudiyil, was ordained on March 12, 2006. I was not invited to take any part in either of these historic occasions of the Catholic Church (however, the Miao Diocese intelligently allowed my eldest daughter, Chaman Wanglat, to read words of God from the Holy Bible). The Itanagar Diocese organizers did not even provide me a seat; forget about inviting me to the podium to speak, while late Tadar Taniang, to whom I was the godfather, was made the master of ceremonies with Gegong Apang (the active persecutor of Christian churches and founder of Donyi-Polo Mission) as the chief guest. The ordination was less of spirituality and more of political activism.

Christianity continued to grow by leaps and bounds in spite of anti-Christian activism under the direct supervision of the chief ministers of the state along with the blessings of North Block, Government of India.

4

RELIGIOUS POLICY OF THE ADMINISTRATION AND ITS IMPLEMENTATION

Let us look at how it all began. Strange as it may sound to you, when India won her independence, the Christian community in Arunachal Pradesh lost theirs. While India passed a beautiful constitution, the Christian community of Arunachal Pradesh lost certain basic freedoms that every human being has a right to: the freedom of religion and the freedom to profess a religion of one's choice and to propagate it, which the constitution guarantees. Self-appointed guardians of Arunachalee culture came from outside Arunachal Pradesh, and the local people were mere observers.

The Home Ministry of the Government of India, in the Union Cabinet decision of 1954, not to allow Christian Missionaries to enter the North-East Frontier Tracts, formulated a policy. The obvious reason could be the outbreak at that time of a demand for an independent sovereign state by the Naga freedom movement of Phizo. The suspicion was given legitimacy by the slogan used by the Naga insurgent movement, "Nagaland for Christ," while seeking a sovereign state.

Prime Minister Jawaharlal Nehru was also advised by the anthropologist-cum-administrator-cum-philosopher, Dr. Verrier Elwin, to stop Christian missionaries from entering NEFA and to defeat the movement built by Reverend David Scot, the infamous pro-Naga movement English preacher who was subsequently expelled from India. This doctrine was carried out with missionary zeal by the then Chief Commissioner (later the Lt. Governor) K. A. A. Raja and the council of ministers.

In all fairness, we must admit that the early framers of a policy for NEFA meant well. In his book *Philosophy for NEFA*, Dr. Verrier Elwin formulated the policy that was wholeheartedly accepted and supported by Pandit Nehru, and it was proposed as the Gospel for the NEFA administration. However, the book was too poetical to be practical. All that the anthropologist author said in one part of the book was contradicted by the norms given by the practical administrator in another part of the same book. There was no consistency, except perhaps in the sincere love that Mr. Elwin had for the tribal people.

The NEFA Administration designed its administrative policies based on Prime Minister Jawaharlal Nehru's five fundamental principles for tribal development:

1. People should be allowed to develop along the lines of their own genius, and we should avoid imposing anything on them. We should try to encourage in every way their own traditional arts and culture.
2. Tribal rights in land and forests should be respected.
3. We should try to train and build up a team of their own people to do work of administration and development.

Some technical personnel from outside will, no doubt, be needed, especially in the beginning. But we should avoid introducing too many outsiders into tribal territory.
4. We should not over-administer these areas or overwhelm them with a multiplicity of schemes. We should rather work through, and not in rivalry to, their own social and cultural institutions.
5. We should judge results, not by statistics or the amount of money spent, but by the quality of human character that is evolved.

The policy makers wanted the tribal religions to be protected. The administration, Dr. Elwin believed, observed a policy of strict religious neutrality and would not impose even tribal religions on those who did not want them.

In the actual implementation of the *Philosophy for NEFA*, however, we notice five distinct phases or traits:

a) A genuine concern for the preservation and fostering of tribal cultures
b) An eagerness to isolate NEFA from any outside influence (isolation is the solution for growth and progress as propagated by the socialistic form of governance)
c) An effort at Indianizing the tribal people by bringing them into the mainstream
d) An attempt at Hinduisation of the tribals, feeling certain that that would be the best way to Indianize them
e) A systematic effort to block even the least Christian influence from penetrating the state, combined with an attempt to suppress the Christian community already in existence in NEFA

The government of the day in Arunachal Pradesh was overzealous and went overboard in implementing the philosophy. In October 1972, the Pradesh Council went to the extent of passing a resolution that stated that "a person belonging to any indigenous tribal community of Arunachal Pradesh who renounces the traditional belief and/or faiths should be deemed to have deserted the community or tribe and to have forfeited all facilities, benefits, advantages, considerations deriving from his/her being a member of that tribe/community." The architect of this resolution, under the advice of the then Lt. Governor K. A. A. Raja, was Late Tomo Riba. (At a later stage, he became a very good friend and an associate in floating a regional political party in 1978 with Late Bakin Partin and Late Oken Lego.) I would, however, be failing my duty if I did not record the fact that it was Tomo Riba who vehemently opposed the Arunachal Pradesh Freedom of Religion Act of 1978 on the floor of the Assembly House. He warned that P. K. Thungon and his party would be squarely responsible for creating a black spot in the history of Arunachal Pradesh and that posterity would judge them. Opposing the Act, he and the entire Peoples Party of Arunachal Pradesh legislature walked out of the House.

In 1976, the Arunachal Pradesh Development cum Cultural Convention held at Pasighat under the leadership of Chief Minister P. K. Thungon passed a resolution on similar lines, requesting the Government of Arunachal Pradesh to take immediate steps to safeguard the indigenous faith and culture of various tribes. (P. K. Thungon, later on, became a Union Minister in both the Indira Gandhi and Narasimha Rao governments. He was subsequently arrested and convicted for corruption and sent to Tihar Jail.) During this convention, the Congress Party was floated with Gora Partin as the Arunachal Pradesh Congress Committee President and C. K. Manpong as the Youth Congress

President. However, after the defeat of the Congress Party in 1977, Chief Minister P. K. Thungon and the entire state Congress Government merged en bloc with the Janata Party and enacted the Freedom of Religion Bill, which became an Act after the President of India assented under the advice of Morarji Desai's Council of Ministers.

The Legislative Assembly of Arunachal Pradesh in 1978 unanimously adopted a private member's resolution by Aken Lego, urging the government to take immediate legislative measures on the basis of the resolution passed by the then Pradesh Council in 1972. It reads: "This assembly resolves that a full-fledged government department for cultural affairs be set up and the resolutions adopted by the Pradesh Council on 5th Oct 1972 and the Cultural Convention in 1976 should urgently be implemented with a view to promoting and maintaining the age-old cultural heritage of the territory."

The assembly passed the Arunachal Pradesh Freedom of Religion Bill in 1978 "to provide for prohibition of conversion from one religious faith to any other religious faith by use of force or inducement or by fraudulent means." The Act makes conversion a cognizable offense punishable with two years' imprisonment and a fine for anyone who attempts to convert a tribal person to any other religion by fraud, inducement, or deceit.

The Arunachal Pradesh Freedom of Religion Bill was directly aimed at preventing people from converting to Christianity. The notorious bill was enacted as an Act by the state government under the leadership of P. K. Thungon and assented by the President of India. Subsequently, the Gegong Apang government rigorously continued the anti-Christian policy.

You can see how a good idea got vitiated in vicious hands. There is nothing as commendable as a genuine concern for the preservation and fostering of tribal cultures. But the idea of isolation was neither good in itself nor practical when it came to implementation.

The whole set of administrators were outsiders, and teachers, skilled workers, and technicians of all sorts were all from non-tribal societies. Harish Chandola, a journalist, wrote, "Why is the inner line there today? I am afraid it is there to prevent thinking people from going in. Otherwise I have known most objectionable characters taken in."

Next, the effort of bringing the tribal people into the national mainstream vitiated into an attempt at Hinduising them. It must be stated that none of the tribes of Arunachal Pradesh have a Hindu background, except for the Nocte (Naga) King's or the Ang, and few smaller clans/tribes. Anthropologists of any worth have testified to the fact. Dr. Elwin even felt that the tribals were somewhat inclined toward Christianity. But a whole lot of literature was produced to prove that the tribal gods were, in reality, Hindu gods, and an effort was made to link the history of each tribe with Hindu mythological figures and stories.

It is believed that after the humiliating defeat in the war with China in 1962, Jawaharlal Nehru embarked upon "Operation NEFA." Goods trains were loaded with old artifacts and remnants from ancient Hindu temples and Indian civilization sites in various parts of the country and sent to NEFA to be placed in important venerable places to give the impression that the Hindu religion and culture existed there throughout the history of NEFA, thereby countering the claim of China that NEFA was part of China. The Department of Archaeology and the Surveyor General of India were given the task of conducting the operation.

Prime Minister Indira Gandhi later followed her father's misconceived policy, and she went a step further by allowing the Rashtriya Swayamsevak Sangh organization to enter NEFA through various NGOs. It is believed that she approved the activation of Akhil Bharatiya Vidyarthi Parishad and Vishwa Hindu Parishad, in NEFA. Indira Gandhi in her desire to bring the aborigines of NEFA into the so called "national main stream" she unknowingly became the guardian angel for the RSS. In an interview with Karan Thapar in the program To the Point on India Today, former Governor T. V. Rajeswar said, "Not only they (RSS) were supportive of this, they wanted to establish contact apart from Mrs. Gandhi, with Sanjay Gandhi also."

As a result of this bonhomie between Prime Minister Indira Gandhi and the RSS, the Home Ministry of the Government of India implemented a policy known as "India is my home" for the youth of NEFA. Prospective young leadership was identified and sent to Bombay to live and study in homes of private influential hard-core Hindu families. All the foster parents were staunch RSS or Vishwa Hindu Parishad members. Notable among them was film actor Asha Parekh. As history would have it, 90 percent of such young leaders (some of whom became IAS officers, politicians, and technocrats) did not become Hindus. If they or the people of the state did not become Hindus, it is because they just did not want to. Dr. Elwin had enough perception to admit years ago that one could not expect people of Arunachal Pradesh to accept Hinduism in a serious manner.

Gradually, another surprising phenomenon began to take root in NEFA. The tribes that followed animist beliefs began to form institutions and places of worship. They put up images of gods and goddesses, which had never existed before, in these so-called temples and even introduced customs akin to Hinduism. Traditionally, none of the indigenous people in NEFA had a formalized institutional place of worship. They worshipped the moon, the sun, and the sky at different sacred landmarks that had no physical structures. The indigenous people would select a date every year for community worship to drive away evil forces or spirits and to seek a good harvest and blessings. The objective of RSS, VHP, North Block, and Late Col. K. A. A. Raja of bringing the indigenous people of NEFA into the national mainstream was thus achieved by formation of institutionalized indigenous animist faith and belief. However, despite support and encouragement (financial help and enactment of a law to support such a recently created institution), the 2011 Census indicates that only 26 percent of Arunachalee still believed in the traditional animist form of worship.

The Hinduisation process went further ahead. Hindu temples were allowed to be built at government expense. Institutions in Assam, Calcutta, and Bombay were subsidized for giving Hindu education to tribal children. Hindu festivals were observed, and pujas were offered at the behest of the local government while our constitution speaks otherwise.

At the same time, Christian priests or pastors were neither allowed to enter Arunachal Pradesh nor could a place of worship be constructed by the local Christians, who constituted less then 1% (percent) of the population as per the 1961 census. There is substantial evidence to show that the state's bureaucrats portrayed Christianity to be a foreign religion and convinced the local political and tribal leaders that Christians were alien to local faiths and beliefs and that they were being used by foreign governments to convert the indigenous people by devious means. This encouraged the local leadership to persecute Christians with impunity. The manner in which the administration, with tacit support from the Government of India, persecuted Christians was shameful and violated their fundamental right of freedom to practice and profess their faith.

5

CHRONICLE OF PERSECUTION

The church grew from strength to strength despite institutionalized persecution against simple and innocent Arunachalee. P. K. Thungon, with the blessing of Chief Commissioner K. A. A. Raja began persecution of Christians with the help of student unions, panchayats, agency councilors, and village authorities. To give legitimacy to the unconstitutional and illegal persecution, P. K. Thungon adopted a resolution on May 18, 1978, in line with the resolutions adopted earlier by the Pradesh Council on October 5, 1972. The Pasighat Convention resolution stated that any person belonging to any of the indigenous tribes and communities of Arunachal Pradesh, who renounces the indigenous belief and faith, should be deemed to have deserted the community and should forfeit the facilities, benefits, advantages, and considerations deriving from his or her being a member of that tribe or community. The resolution also urged the Government of Arunachal Pradesh to take immediate and effective steps for implementation of the resolution. Any students accepting Christianity were to be deprived of post-matric and post-secondary stipends, the stipend of Rs. 75

per month in lieu of rations, and the special preference given to Arunachal tribal contractors of 7½ percent would be stopped.

Most of the government officers like District Commissioners, Extra Assistant Commissioners, Circle Officers, and other officials took an active part in the persecution of Christians in Arunachal Pradesh.

January 7, 1969: Harbans Singh, Home Guard Commander, ordered his subordinates to burn down churches in Deed, Dem, and Neelam villages in Ziro area. The DC, Subansiri District, was informed of the persecution, but he refused to take any cognizance of the crimes committed by his subordinates. B. K. Nehru, Governor of Assam, who was the Administrator of NEFA on behalf of the President of India, was also informed by a delegation of the North East India Christian Council, but interestingly, he only gave verbal assurance that such incidents would not happen again. Nothing was done to stop the persecution.

May 6, 1969: The DC, Khonsa, Tirap Division, sent a police inspector to the villages of Longwi, Khamkhai, Kjamlang, and Kharsang to threaten the Christians and warn the people thinking of becoming Christians that the NEFA government is likely to arrest them if they become Christians.

April 5, 1970: At Nampong, the DC, Khonsa, arrested Dikay Murang, Samman Murang, and Yonglim Taikam of Khamkhai village, because they had become Christians.

August 8, 1970: L. N. Kumar De, DC, Siang Dist., Along, issued an externment order to Tai Tatu, an Adi of Ngsi village, Tirbin area, as his activities were considered to be against the culture and religious pursuits of the Adi people. Tai Tatu was a Christian and was prohibited from practicing his religion and was continuously threatened. No protection was given to him, and finally, the government asked him to leave his own area.

October 22, 1970: At Dipa village, Along, the Circle Officer, Dagmo Zini, led a group of people who threatened the local Christians, forcing them to put their thumb impressions to a statement that stated that they have renounced their Christian religion. Christians were threatened of having their properties confiscated and of being driven from the village if they kept their Christian religion. After this, the Circle Officer (APCS Junior Administration) gave an order to pull down the church, and it was burnt.

October 26–28, 1970: At Dipa village, Along, anti-Christian lectures and demonstrations were carried on October 26 and 27, and then on October 28, the local church was destroyed on the order of Dagmo Zini, Circle Officer (APCS Junior Administration).

October 29, 1970: Dagmo Zini, Circle Officer (APCS Junior Administration) and his party went to Zipoo village, Along. They delivered anti-Christian lectures at Magi and Dipa villages. They destroyed the local church building and desecrated the Holy Bible.

October 31 to November 2, 1970: At Likabali village, Along, public meetings were held. The purpose of the meetings was clearly to give anti-Christian lectures. Many government officers were present throughout these meetings. On November 2, the topic of the meeting was how to prevent Christians from entering NEFA. Various leaders spoke against the Christian religion. Disparaging remarks were made publicly about anyone leaving their ancestral religion to join the Christian religion. A resolution was passed stating that whoever accepted Christianity would be fined Rs. 2,000 and be subject to imprisonment.

December 30, 1970: At Miao village, the Government arrested Khiran Chamchang, Kanwan Chamchang, and Mitchin Murang of Kharsang village as they were Christian leaders. At Nampong village, the Government arrested Thakna Taikam and Kengi Murang for being Christians.

January 9, 1971: On January 5, 1971, a group of people, both Christians and non-Christians, petitioned the Deputy Commissioner, Khonsa, to meet them at Miao on January 9 regarding the five men arrested from Miao and Nampong villages. But no government authority at Miao would give them a hearing on that date.

Jagir Singh, Extra Assistant Commissioner, Sagalee, went on an all-out assault on Christians in the area. He ordered villagers and panchayat members to assault Christians, including pastors, and burn down their houses. Orders were given by him to set churches on fire and to shut them down. On February 20, 1969, Jagir Singh forced panchayat members led by Nabum Lilu and Tasar Taram to set fire to the Rach and Peri churches. On February 24, 1971, he threatened all the Christians in the Sagalee area that they would be punished if they refused to give up their Holy Bibles. He seized Bibles from villagers and burnt them. Those who did not comply with his orders were beaten up, and their Bibles were forcibly taken away. Later, when Jagir Singh was the DC, Pasighat, he ordered the destruction of a church in East Siang.

February 6, 1972: After getting assurance from the DC, Ziro, Tasar Mangha beat up Bebiang Bingcho for being a Christian. On the same day Ms. Lengbia Yapu, a grown-up girl, was cut with the blunt side of a *dao* (a traditional weapon of the Nyishis) and stripped completely naked before the public. The girl was bought to the DC's office by both Christian and non-Christian people for justice. But the DC did not take any action against Tasar Mangha.

March 9, 1972: Dr. A. C. Hazarika of Sagalee Hospital came to Karoi village. He told the Christian people that "no medicines will be given to the Christian people." In the evening, he dragged out the Christians including women and children from their houses and forced them to stay outside their homes for the whole night.

May 8, 1972: A group of Baptist Christians was asked by the Subansiri Panchayat to attend their meetings at Ziro. They were tied to the ground where leeches and ants fed on them. They bled from their mouths, noses, and ears. They were asked to carry stones around their necks as a punishment. Whenever they refused to do so, the panchayat personnel loaded their belongings on them and made them work as their servants. During mealtimes, their hands were tied to posts, and then they were asked to eat their food like animals without using their hands. They were kept as prisoners; they were sent to different places and made to work as servants without any remuneration or proper food. Their relatives approached T. C. Hazarika, Deputy Comissioner, for justice and demanded that they be set free. But each time, he turned his face away from them. (The Subansiri Baptist Christian Council informed this incident to me, as I was the Chairman of the Arunachal Christian Action Committee.)

In 1974, B. Kumar, Extra Assistant Commissioner, Sagalee, ordered Teli Ekhu of Khemti village to be beaten up for not renouncing Christianity. When she reported this to Nyishi Christian leaders, she was summoned to his office where Techi Teki, Zilla Parishad member, stripped her and hung her upside down in public and molested her. Nabam Boki of Bobia village was abused and insulted by Techi Teki when he refused to renounce his Christian faith. B. Kumar ordered Techi Tulo and Techi Tara of Karoi village to retract statements given by them to Christian leaders about losses suffered during persecution by villagers and had them hung by their hands for eleven hours when they refused. They were also made to put their thumb impressions on pieces of paper whose contents they did not know and fined two *mithuns*. Similarly, Nyair Jil of Khat village was made to put his thumb impression on a statement saying that what he had reported to Christian leaders about his losses was false and Nabam Tara of Khat village was fined one *mithun* for reporting his losses and for refusing to deny his faith. Teli Tagam, a Christian of Rangajan village in Assam, who had come for some work at the Extra Assitant Commissioner's office, was beaten up severely by Techi Takar.

All the above-quoted incidents pale before the horrors of 1974. The Government put the panchayats, student organizations, and cultural societies into action. Money meant for the promotion of culture and student welfare was used for building a civilian army of volunteers who organized anti-Christian demonstrations and indulged in anti-Christian violence. The instances are too many to be quoted. But the leading criminals claimed they had clear orders from K. A. A. Raja, the chief commissioner of Arunachal Pradesh.

As per records, forty-four Baptist churches were either physically destroyed or burnt down between February and June 1974, and of these, thirty-two churches were destroyed in the month of April 1974 alone. To name a few:

April 18, 1974: Pang Baptist church
April 20, 1974: Khemty, Sito, Tepi, Rach Baptist churches
April 24, 1974: Bobia, Lidin, Tabi, Lema Baptist churches
April 29, 1974: Khil, Chulyu, Joram Baptist churches

The persecutors also destroyed or burnt 103 Christian homes in 1974, including those of Khoda Tana, Nabom Rungkhi, Tana Epa, Ter Tana, Techi Togun, Techi Eppo, Taba Jabor, Lishi Bagi,

Tana Sera, and Teli Chach. Not satisfied with the burning and destruction of homes, 109 Christians were physically assaulted, tortured, or kidnapped during the 1974 persecutions. 192 granary storehouses along with food grains and traditional utensils and ornaments were reduced to ashes or looted.

K. A. A. Raja used Tadar Tang, Councillor, who subsequently became a minister, to persecute Christians. Nabom Rungkhi, who was extensively persecuted, wrote a letter to the prime minister and to the Christian Council of India seeking protection and relief and forwarded a separate letter to K. A. A. Raja on May 7, 1975. K. A. A. Raja, who was the architect of persecution, replied to Rungkhi's letter on May 17, 1975, informing him that his petition had been forwarded to Tadar Tang and directing him to henceforth take up the matter with the latter. It is interesting to note that K. A. A. Raja specifically stated, "I, as the Administrator, will not involve myself in such cases." His statement implied that as an administrator, he would not safeguard the persecuted people of Arunachal Pradesh when their constitutional rights were denied with impunity.

Tadar Tang on his part wrote a letter to Nabom Rungkhi on June 3, 1975, urging him to come to Itanagar, assuring him of his safety with a cynical note: "I may be wrong in thinking so, but circumstances now make me believe that you are playing in the hands of vested interests who do not wish well either of our community or of India. The early you understand their designs in the matter it would be for all of us." I believe the above sentence implied that Rungkhi should denounce his Christian faith and revert to animist beliefs. For those who may not know who Tadar Tang is, the following paragraph will give you an idea.

Tadar Tang had a very long political inning among the Nyishi tribe of Arunachal Pradesh. He joined politics as a panchayat member in the early 1970s. He rose up to become a cabinet minister in both Thungon's and Apong's governments. As a person, he was very sober and a good friend of mine. His educational qualifications were his liability. As a result, people took advantage of his simplicity and tribal innocence. I believe it is possible K. A. A. Raja saw this vulnerability and took advantage by encouraging him to lead the persecution of Christians in the Nyishi stronghold. Tadar Tang later came under the scanner of the CBI and was convicted in the rape seed oil scandal.

During the 1980s, T. L Rajkumar was a tyrant in Tirap District of Arunachal Pradesh (which included the present Longding and Changlang Districts). He was the speaker of the state assembly and a member of the ruling party and, together with Gegong Apang, the then Chief Minister, carried out systematic persecution against Christians of the District by getting them arrested and churches were burned under his direct directions. He was an absolute ruler unrestrained by the constitution and laws of our country. Plato and Aristotle define a tyrant as "one who rules without law, and uses extreme and cruel tactics—against his own people as well as others".

T. L. Rajkumar ordered burning down of the Catholic Church in Moktuwa village on May 5, 1981 at 10 am. He was very angry for not being able to burn down Borduria village church in 1979 and his grudge manifested itself in the destruction of Moktuwa church where Tero Kakho was the official Catholic catechist under Dibrugarh diocese. Rajkumar used Tewang Lowang and Pilo Kamhua to persecute the Christians of Moktuwa village. Not satisfied with the burning down of the church there, he instructed the Deputy Commissioner, Tirap to arrest Catholic Christian leaders namely Wangkiam Kamhua, Chefa Kamhua and H. W. Atua on June 15, 1981. They were released on bail on July 17,

1981 with the help of lawyers of the Arunachal Christian Action Committee.

It is interesting to note here that both the early chief ministers of Arunachal Pradesh, who rose to their position for being anti-Christian, were arrested on corruption charges. P. K. Thungon, who joined the NEFA service as Circle Officer, became the first chief minister of Arunachal Pradesh and subsequently walked the hallowed halls of parliament to become a Union Minister. He was accused and convicted by the CBI on corruption charges. Similarly, the longest-serving chief minister of Arunachal Pradesh, Gegong Apang, was arrested in August 2010 in the Rs. 1000 Crore Public Distribution System scam.

Gegong Apang institutionalized Donyi Poloism and facilitated Donyi Polo activists', like Talom Rukbo's, participation in national and international conferences on indigenous faith and belief. He lavishly funded the Donyi Polo movement. Persecution against Christians spread throughout the state of Arunachal Pradesh. From early 2000, however, Apang's concept of religious intolerance took a complete U-turn. On March 12, 2006, Gegong Apang was invited as the chief guest on the occasion of the inauguration of the Itanagar Diocese and the installation of Reverend John Thomas Kattrukudiyil as the first bishop of West Arunachal Pradesh. Apang began his address chanting, "Praise the Lord, Praise the Lord, Praise the Lord." He stated that it was a historical day and thanked the Holy Father for creating two Dioceses in Arunachal Pradesh. He also spoke about how "Jesus asked his tormentors to be forgiven" and said Catholics believe in saving the soul as much as the body. He assured the complete support of his government to the church and praised Don Bosco College. He then invited all the archbishops and bishops along with priests and church workers for a tea party in his house.

The government of the day also extensively used student bodies and panchayat members to persecute the Christians of Arunachal Pradesh. For example, Nabum Rebia, the chief secretary, All Subansiri District Students' Union, was used to issue an appeal urging people of Arunachal Pradesh to "understand the foxy motive of the Christian priests when they take our children to their school. We should make all-out effort to stop further conversion to Christianity and reconvert all those who have been converted on account of their not understanding the wicked nature of Christian priests." He ends the appeal by stating, "We must be determined to remove this religion not only from Arunachal Pradesh but from India."

After serving as President of Arunachal Pradesh Students' Union Nabum, Rebia joined electoral politics and was unsuccessful initially (his elder brother, Nabum Atum, an active Christian persecutor in the 1970s and 1980s, also contested elections but was rejected by the Nyishi electorate). Nabum Rebia was picked up by Gegong Apang, who nominated him to the Rajya Sabha as MP for twelve long years (from 1996 to 2008). Subsequently, he was given a Congress party ticket to contest the Doimukh Assembly Constituency, which he won in 2009. He was appointed as Parliamentary Secretary by Dorjee Khandu as the speaker of the assembly in 2014 by Nabum Tuki, who happens to be his cousin brother; and as a minister by Pema Khandu. The majority of Rebia's relatives have converted to various Christian denominations while he and his family continue to believe in the Donyi Polo faith.

Earlier in April 1974, some students of Doimukh Government Higher Secondary School led by Nabum Rebia, Nabum Atum, Tao Tania, and Tarin Dakpe along with Tana Epo, Zilla Parishad member from the Sagalee area, unleashed a reign of terror with systematic physical assault of Christians, burning and looting of their homes, and burning and destruction of churches. Doimukh Government Higher Secondary School and the villages that were attacked by these students are situated in close proximity to Naharlagun, which was the temporary capital of Arunachal Pradesh, and the incidents took place under the very nose of the administration.

Leave aside poor, innocent, and illiterate villages, even educated people were not spared by the persecutors.

Khoda Tana, whose house was burnt down in 1974, went to the office of A. Bagchi, Circle Officer, to request him to stop the persecution of villagers in Doimukh, but he was rebuked and was confined in Nabam Tada's house for one week without any food. During his school days, Khoda Tana was arrested by P. N. Kaul, Base Superintendent, Kimin, in 1958 when he was going home to his village Rei in Sagalee from John Firth Mission School in North Lakhimpur, Assam. His Bible and hymnbooks were taken away, and he was ordered not to go back to the Christian Mission School. Khoda Tana was sent to CRPF custody for three days. He was then handed over to Hage Ekha, Gaon Bura of Hari village, to work as his slave for a week. After this, he was sent to Tezu to study in the government school there. Khoda Tana later graduated from J. N. College, Pasighat, and joined government service in the NEFA Civil Secretariat. In 1978, he resigned from his government job to devote his time to spread the Gospel. He served as Secretary, President, and Treasurer of the Nyishi Baptist Church Council.

The Deputy Commissioner, Ziro, arrested Neelam Taram, a student at the time, on July 2, 1972, when he urged the Deputy Commissioner to ensure that persecution of Christians is stopped. He was released seven days later on the intervention of C. Gohain, the MP from Arunachal Pradesh. On January 6, 1974, on his way to Doimukh, Neelam Taram and Toko Taba were caught and beaten up severely by Techi Teki on the orders of Tadar Tang in the Inspection Bungalow, Sagalee. Neelam Taram graduated from J. N. College, Pasighat. He was a founding member of the erstwhile Nyishi Baptist Christian Convention and was its president. He was then elected President of Subansiri Baptist Christian Association and was a founding member of the Arunachal Christian Forum. He entered electoral politics and became an MLA in 1990 and was appointed as Minister for Civil Supplies. He went on to become the Minister of Home Affairs, a post he held from 1991 to 1996. He was later elected as the leader of the Congress Legislature Party and served as the Leader of the Opposition from 1996 to 1999.

No effective steps were taken by the administration at any level to punish the criminals during the persecution. But the more the Christians were made to suffer, the more the Christian community grew. So it dawned on the authorities of Arunachal Pradesh that the only way to prevent further growth of the Church was to make conversion itself illegal. Therefore, the Arunachal Pradesh Freedom of Religion Bill 1978 was enacted. The District Commissioners of the five districts of Arunachal Pradesh would administer the acid test to verify the genuineness of religious conversion. This was the progress that secular India had made!

6

CONSECRATION OF THE FIRST CATHOLIC CHURCH IN ARUNACHAL PRADESH

Borduria is considered to be the crucible from which the Catholic faith grew and spread throughout NEFA. It was from here that Bishop Kerketta, SDB, and Fr. Thomas Menamparampil, SDB, initiated mission work to introduce the Catholic faith and to spread the good news to the state of Arunachal Pradesh. They established direct contact with the tribes of undivided Tirap District and the Nyishi and the Apatani in the west.

In 1975, I happened to go to Don Bosco Technical School, Shillong, seeking admission for my younger brother Wangdung. Though the admission period was over, the wise Fr. Thomas accepted my brother as he was from a new tribe of Northeast India. The following year I managed to get admission for two more boys, Tero Kakho and late Ranlam Dada. Before they were admitted, Fr. Thomas asked me if I had any objection if the students were to accept the Catholic Christian faith. Although I was not a Christian at that time, I was reasonably versed with

Christianity from my early education in Christian schools and informed him that I had no objection if they accepted Christ on their own free will. Subsequently, Wangdung and Denis Tero Kakho were baptized in 1976 and late Albert Ranlam Dada in 1977 at Don Bosco Chapel, Shillong.

When Bishop Kerketta, SDB, and Fr. Thomas, SDB, realized that the Arunachalee had an open mind to Christianity, they decided to enter the Union Territory for an assessment. I was requested to arrange an Inner Line Permit for Fr. Thomas. Since the local administration was hostile to any Christian priests or pastors, I applied for the Inner Line Permit from the district authorities for him not as a priest but using his official designation, and surprisingly the Inner Line Permit was issued in the name of M. C. Thomas, Director of Don Bosco Technical Institute, Shillong, which was legally and technically correct.

Fr. Thomas arrived in Borduria via Dibrugarh on August 17, 1978. On the next day, he and I proceeded for Longding, in the Wancho area, after spending a night at Borduria village. On the way to Longding, our hired vehicle met with an accident with an army truck at Kapu village. Nothing happened to me, but Fr. Thomas broke his leg (the patella was crushed to pieces). The Longding trip had to be abandoned, and we had to return to Borduria via Khonsa General Hospital. The doctors from the hospital advised me to take Fr. Thomas to Dibrugarh immediately for further treatment. On my request, the District Medical Officer provided an ambulance against payment. I am indebted to the DMO and all the doctors and nurses of Khonsa General Hospital.

On our way to Dibrugarh, Fr. Thomas requested me if he could halt for a few minutes to go to the washroom and to say prayers in my village house (just about a hundred meters from the KBJ Road, now NH 315A) before proceeding to Dibrugarh. When we reached my house, Fr. Thomas requested me if he could baptize me along with my two children, Marcus Soomwang and Christine Chaman. He told me it would be a historic moment in the church's history.

Although I had studied comparative world religion as well as the Bible in Mount Hermon School, Darjeeling, in the 1960s, I was taken aback by such a request from the injured priest. Fr. Thomas said he wanted to follow the footsteps of Jesus and that it was through the passion of Jesus that we are redeemed. If I allowed him to perform his priestly duty, it would be his greatest gift from the Arunachal Pradesh visit. I was confused, but I just could not refuse the request of an injured and suffering priest. At the same time, I strongly felt that it would be a challenge to Chief Minister P. K. Thungon's Arunachal Pradesh Freedom of Religion Act 1978. I agreed to get baptized into the Catholic Christian faith along with my children on August 18, 1978. This was the first Catholic baptism to have been performed by an ordained priest inside the state of Arunachal Pradesh, and as such, the first Catholic family was born in the state.

For Fr. Thomas, who later on became the archbishop, it was a historic occasion as he was the first Salesian priest to visit Arunachal Pradesh legally with an Inner Line Permit issued by the Deputy Commissioner, Tirap. Let us remember that this historical event had taken place where conversion to Christianity was considered as anti-national by the state government. It had enacted the Arunachal Pradesh Freedom of Religion Act 1978 and erected a "bamboo curtain" resembling the iron curtain of the USSR to isolate the state from any outside influence.

Growth of the Catholic Church in Arunachal Pradesh began with a beautiful crucifix gifted to me by Fr. Rubio. The crucifix was kept in my residence, which was the meeting place for prayer and worship of a few Catholics (about ten families) in Borduria, Tirap District.

To fulfill the spiritual needs of our faith; we decided to build a small Catholic church inside my house compound. Ninety-five percent of Borduria's villagers, none of whom were Catholic or Christians at that point in time, offered a helping hand to build the 15-feet-by-30-feet church without asking for any remuneration. Although the Arunachal Pradesh Freedom of Religion Act 1978 was in full operation at that time, the Borduria church was built with great fanfare. The construction began on April 10, 1979. I never could dream that a family chapel would turn into the first Catholic church of Arunachal Pradesh to be officially blessed by bishops along with priests and nuns. In May 1979, the crucifix was solemnly taken from my house to the newly constructed church in a candlelight procession in readiness for the blessing of the church.

Tension had been mounting from the time the construction of the church started. The State Government instigated a group of people from the same village to oppose the construction of the church. Wanglin Lowangdong, the chief of Borduria, now MLA, was encouraged by the then government to oppose its construction. To strengthen Wanglin's hand, N. Namati, the then Education Minister, and former Chief Minister Gegong Apang arrived at Khonsa to strategize the demolition of the new church in Borduria. A huge sum of money was earmarked from the NBF fund, and they conducted a meeting at the Khonsa Town Club. Four buffalos and a few pigs were slaughtered for a feast with plenty of liquor for those attending the meeting. Wanglin exhorted the people to take up arms and proceed to Borduria village (his own village) to demolish the Catholic Church.

Among the important personalities who attended this meeting were T. L. Rajkumar (he has been a minister and a speaker in the state for more than twenty years); chiefs from most of the villages in the Nocte area and some chiefs from the Wancho area; Tedian Lowang, then Vice President of the Zilla Parishad (now a Catholic); Wangkop Lowang, Political Assistant (now converted to Baptist Christian); Wangmai Rajkumar, officiating chief of Namsang; Wangpha Lowang, former Minister; K. T. Longchang, MLA; and N. Namati, minister. Since the government patronized this meeting, the chiefs, gaon burahs, and panchayat leaders represented most of the villages from the Nocte and Wancho area.

When the chief of Chanu, Panwang Wangham, realized that this meeting was for attacking Borduria village, he rose up from his chair and proclaimed that never in the history of Changjen or Ngauzen (a cluster of villages under the authority of the Chanu Chief and another cluster of villages under the Ngaunu Chief) would they even dream of attacking the mighty *"Tsa-Laa"* or *"Lanu,"* meaning "father of all villages." He then walked out of the meeting, and all the other smaller chiefs followed him. The attempt to destroy the Catholic Church in Borduria thus failed. The actions of Panwang Wangham, the chief of Chanu, prevented the bloodshed and mayhem that would have ensued if attempts were made to destroy the Borduria church.

With the passage of time, the anti-Christian movement gradually faded away with even Wanglin Lowangdong joining the Baptist Christian Church on December 29, 1991. He helped the formation of the Tirap Baptist Church Council (TBCC was funded and administered by the Ao Baptist Church of Nagaland) to construct the Baptist Church in Borduria. The Baptist Church has grown manyfold in Tirap District under the patronization of Wanglin.

The dedication of the Catholic Church in Borduria was fixed for August 2, 1979, but who would bless it? Being the first Catholic Church in Arunachal Pradesh, it had to be done with full solemnity, but bishops and priests were not permitted to enter Arunachal Pradesh. The sequence of events that took place culminating in the consecration of the church is given below:

> July 16, 1979: The Chairman of Arunachal Christian Action Committee officially requested permission from the Deputy Commissioner, Tirap, for five priests and two sisters to visit the village for the blessing of Borduria Catholic Church.
>
> July 20, 1979: The DC informed me to "wait, we will see."
>
> July 20–25, 1979: Fr. Kallarackal Job, SDB, trained a group of Nocte students at Naharkatiya, Assam, to prepare for the blessing of the church.
>
> July 15 and 23, 1979: Two ministers were sent to Khonsa to strategize how to destroy the Borduria Catholic Church.
>
> July 21, 1979: The chief of Borduria and his group planned to destroy Borduria Catholic Church, but the meeting at Khonsa Town Club failed because most of the village chiefs of Tirap District refused to attack Borduria village to destroy the church and walked out of the meeting en masse.
>
> July 21, 1979: I received a letter no. IL 2/79/86 from the Deputy Commissioner, Tirap, signed by P. C. Das, EAC, Judicial, stating, "This is to say

that we do not know how Bishops would like to visit Khonsa. This is quite unusual for the church dignitaries like them. Please, therefore, let us know the purpose to be visited by each of the nine persons."

July 23, 1979: I replied, "I am here to inform you that the two bishops and the church leaders have been invited by the Chairman of the Tirap Catholic Association on the occasion of *"Hum-Wang"* (blessing) ceremony of a Catholic Church at Borduria. They would like to visit Borduria and Khonsa. Rev. Fr. Kallarackal would like to come on 28th July 1979 in advance to oversee the arrangements and accommodation, etc." (signed by L. Wanglat, Chairman of Christian Action Committee).

July 24, 1979: I received a letter no. IL/2/79/88 from DC, Khonsa, stating, "This is to inform you that construction of a place of worship normally requires government's prior permission. It is not known as to where it is made. Therefore you are requested to please let this office know when the church was made, who donated the land and what the present area is."

In reply to this letter, I personally went to Khonsa to meet the DC, Tirap, in person. The DC, late J. M. Syiem, told me that he will have to consult Itanagar and would inform me accordingly.

July 24, 1979: Another request was sent to DC, Tirap, signed by 124 families of Borduria village.

In the meantime, the chief of Borduria and Tedian Lowang, then Vice President, Tirap Zilla

Parishad (now a Catholic convert), along with a few panchayat members tried to stir up the people against the Borduria Catholics. They took thumb impressions on blank sheets of paper from unsuspecting villagers and on its strength requested the deputy commissioner not to issue Inner Line Permits to the Catholic priests, nuns, and two bishops.

July 27, 1979: Political Assistant Officer, Wangkap Lowang, father of T. L. Rajkumar, (anti-Christian and persecutor before he converted to the Baptist Church) came to the village to inform us that no Inner Line Permits would be issued to the Catholic priests and nuns based on the objection by Wanglin Lowangdong, the chief of Borduria, and his supporters. At that time, Wangkap Lowang was a highly regarded Hindu activist who used to perform pujas for individuals and communities. (Interestingly, after the death of his wife and his youngest late son Ajoy Rajkumar, he too accepted Christ and joined the Baptist Church.) After the visit of Wangkap Lowang, 95 percent of Borduria villagers had a meeting and passed a resolution opposing Wanglin Lowangdong, the chief of Borduria, and formed an organization known as Tangchi Nadi Association. All the villagers who were not Christians decided to request the bishop of Dibrugarh to accept them in the Holy Catholic Church as new members.

July 28, 1979: A group of forty representatives from Borduria, Kamai, Laptang, Lothong,

Lapnan, Paniduria, Tupi, Dadam, Lanwang, Wansathong, Sumsi, Kheti, Sabang, Pullong, and Chasa villages went to the DC's office demanding Inner Line Permits for the bishop, priests, and nuns of the Catholic Church, but the DC refused.

July 30, 1979: J. M. Syiem, DC, Tirap, issued an order no. CA.129/79/19: "Whereas a controversy had cropped up regarding the proposed visit of the Bishops and other Roman Catholic priests to Borduria village in connection with the blessing ceremony of the Roman Catholic Church there on 2nd August, the undersigned regrets his inability to issue any inner line pass to them at this stage." On receiving this order, another meeting was held at Borduria village where all the clan leaders of Borduria village stood up one by one and declared that they would attend the consecration of the church and become Christians. Till now, they had supported the Catholic Church as friends but not as co-religionists. The people insisted again and again that they would accept Christ and become Catholics. By the afternoon, the people once again decided to inform the DC, Tirap, that if the permit was not issued the entire village would go down to Naharkatiya and receive baptism. They also said that the public of Borduria would proceed to the check gate and bring in the bishops, priests, and nuns by using force if necessary.

July 31, 1979: In the morning, DC, Tirap, informed the Borduria Church Committee to come and collect the Inner Line Permits for the bishops, priests, and nuns. The permit was sent to Fr. Kallarackal Job, SDB, at Naharkatiya.

July 31, 1979: Fr. Job, SDB, the newly appointed parish priest for the Tirap mission came to Borduria.

August 1, 1979: At 2:00 p.m., a team led by Bishop Robert Kerketta; Fr. Mathia Kochuparampil, SDB Provincial, Guwahati; Fr. George Pudessery, parish priest of Naharkatiya; Fr. Paulinus Chempalayil of Bishop House, Dibrugarh; Fr. Thomas Menamparampil of Don Bosco, Shillong (who later became the Archbishop of Guwahati); Fr. Chacko Kakkanat of St. Joseph's Seminary, Dibrugarh; Sr. Regis of Little Flower School, Dibrugarh; and Sr. Jacqueline Viegas of St. Mary's School, Dibrugarh, came to Borduria, in the Tirap District of Arunachal Pradesh. Each priest and nun came on a legal Inner Line Permit. This clearly indicated the power of the people in the true spirit of democracy.

August 2, 1979: At 11:15 a.m., Bishop Kerketta along with the priests blessed the small Catholic Church at Borduria. The first Catholic Church in the whole of Arunachal Pradesh was born. After the blessing, a Holy Mass was conducted. Immediately after the mass, hundreds of people thronged before the priests in an orderly line to be baptized. In total, 776 people took baptism in Borduria village during the blessing and consecration of the church.

The 776 indigenous Arunachali people defied the Arunachal Pradesh Freedom of Religion Act

1978 as Indians and citizens of a secular state to choose the religion of their choice. The seed was sown at Borduria for the Catholic Church to freely walk the length and breadth of Arunachal Pradesh and to be free to worship the religion of their choice.

The baptism to the Catholic faith was orderly and was accepted by each individual on his or her own free will. None of them were enticed or induced to become Christians. The bishop and the priests announced through the public address system both in Hindi and Assamese that they should accept baptism only if they wanted to become Christians on their own free will. The blessing of the church was witnessed by K. D. Singh, Superintendent of Police, Tirap; the Extra Assistant Commissioner; the CRPF Commanding Officer, SIB; and SB officers of the Government of India and other officers.

August 2, 1979, was the starting point in the creation of two Dioceses in the state of Arunachal Pradesh after the 1978 anti-conversion law was enacted in Arunachal Pradesh with the blessings of the Janata Party Government of India, New Delhi.

The best way to describe the above scenario would be, in the words of Jesus, "the harvest is great, pray that the Father sends more helpers." The distribution of candles after the baptism had great significance for the people. After communion, without a word from anyone, they entered the church (the service was going on in a temporary *shamiana* just next to the small thatch-roofed church) and put the candles at the feet of Christ. When the priests entered the church to unvest, they could see the beautiful illumination due to all the candles burning before the crucifix. Mothers took their children to drop coins at the feet of Jesus. It was truly a sight to behold. Even the weather held out. The sky remained threatening, but it did not rain.

After mass began the solemn lunch. Rice, meat, and rice beer were served with lavish generosity to all the people present. There was a festive mood among the people, and everything moved forward according to plan. The bishop and the team went around Borduria village after lunch. It was a good climb to the historic village, perched on a rocky hill. The team was greeted with smiling faces everywhere. Though only a few homes were privileged to welcome the bishop's team, in every house there were holy pictures, which gave the impression of it being an old Catholic home. Several children from the village were studying in Catholic schools, and every picture given to them in school had been carefully preserved. The bishop and his team were offered meat and fish cooked in the local style and *"zumin,"* a sweet rice beer. Meanwhile, traditional dances had begun in the field near my house. The people wanted the bishop, the fathers, and the sisters to join in the dances, and the latter readily consented. Night came, and the bishop and his team left for the Khonsa Circuit House where lodging for the bishop, priests, and the nuns had been arranged.

On the third day, there was a meeting with the leaders of the village who asked the bishop for a school and a hospital. The bishop and some of the fathers spoke, congratulating them and promising to do everything possible to help them. The bishop declared that one day Borduria of Tirap District, Arunachal Pradesh, would be the seat of the first bishop of Arunachal Pradesh and a beautiful cathedral would be built. (This, however, was a hollow promise. The Bishop House was taken to Miao, which had less than eighty Catholic families. The Catholics of Borduria Village and Tirap and Longding District were sad but supportive of the Holy See's decision.) The bishop and the others then visited my father, Wangnium Sote Raja, retired *zamadar* and acting chief of Borduria who was, and is still, practicing the Hindu Vaishnavite faith.

At about 2:15 p.m., the delegation left Borduria with joy in their hearts for having achieved the impossible. Fr. Job stayed back for a day to meet the church leaders from other villages. Thus an epoch-making event came to a happy conclusion, "the blessing of the first official Catholic Church in Arunachal Pradesh." The credit for the perfect organization (food, accommodation, lights, mikes, *pandal*, seating, etc.) goes to my mother Senphiak; my wife Tei; brothers Wangdung, Wangman, Wangli, Kamwang, and Wanja; sisters Chate and Chatan; elders and clan leaders of Borduria village; and my team of youths and Don Bosco students.

The significance of Borduria Church is of importance because of the fact that twenty-eight other villages owed their allegiance to the chief of Borduria. Therefore, it was the gateway to the hearts of the people of Arunachal to let Jesus into their families.

Fr. Job Kallarackal, SDB, the first Catholic priest in charge of undivided Tirap Mission, said, "The Lord has worked wonders among us. He had shown once more the power of His Spirit and He will continue to do the same even more powerfully in future. The possibilities are immense. Many villages are enquiring about Christ. Just because there is a strong, powerful and organized opposition, we are sure Christ will conquer. To Him who is able to do so much more than we can even ask for, or even think of, by means of the power working in us: to God be the glory in the Church and in Christ Jesus, for all time and forever, Amen."

On our request, the bishop of Dibrugarh appointed a full-time preacher, Tero Kakho, as a catechist. He was the first indigenous catechist in the Indian state of Arunachal Pradesh to be officially appointed as an active religious member of the Catholic Church. To guide Tero Kakho, the bishop of Dibrugarh appointed Fr. Job, SDB, as the first district mission priest of undivided Tirap. After a year, the Borduria Parish was declared as an independent parish of Dibrugarh Diocese. This parish was the largest in the whole of India. Its jurisdiction included the whole of Longding, Tirap, Changlang, Namsai, Lohit, Dibang Valley, and Anini Districts of East Arunachal Pradesh. With limited resources at his disposal, Fr. Job, SDB, the adventurous and dedicated priest, did tremendous work among the Noctes, Wanchos, Tangsas, Singphos, Khamtis, Mishmis, and Adis.

Earlier, on being repeatedly refused an Inner Line Permit, Fr. Job decided to break the law by proceeding to Nokfan (the first Catholic village in the Wancho area) by boat up the Namrup river (Tissa river in Arunachal Pradesh); accompanied by two nuns and a Catholic youth from Nokfan village, they started their journey upstream. Unfortunately for him and his team, the anti-Christian leaders of Nokfan village reported to the district administration about the Catholic priest conducting church services in their village. The local police went to Nokfan village in strength and conducted a search with arrest warrants. The police team was headed by Sub Inspector O. C. Bhutia (who was promoted as OSD with former Chief Minister Gegong Apang). Fr. Job was arrested and convicted for violation of the Eastern Bengal Frontier Regulations of 1873. He was also the first priest to be convicted under the Arunachal Pradesh Freedom of Religion Act 1978. He was let off with a simple fine. His alleged crime was for being a faithful pastor for Indian Catholics in Arunachal Pradesh and for conducting a holy mass and giving communion to his parishioners.

Fr. Job was replaced by Fr. P. K. George, SDB, who was stationed at Tinsukia with a Bible school to run. Fr. George was the first Catholic priest to live in Borduria village in a humble thatched house as the parish priest of East Arunachal Pradesh. The parish priest's house was constructed on land donated by my family. Presently this plot is being used by the Sisters of the Missionaries of Charity.

In 1992, the Sisters of the Missionaries of Charity entered West Arunachal Pradesh although Brothers of the Missionaries of Charity first entered Borduria, East Arunachal Pradesh, in 1991. Both Brother Mario Das and Brother Anad worked with the sick and the dying for one year. They were also arrested by O. C. Bhutia and removed from Borduria in 1992.

Following the Borduria event, the bishop of Tezpur opened the Harmuti Mission under the dynamic personality of Fr. Kollandai. This mission was handed over to Fr. C. C. Jose, SDB, as parish priest of West Arunachal, Tawang, Bomdila, East Kameng, Upper and Lower Subansiri, and West Siang District, while Fr. P. K. George, SDB, was posted to the Tinsukia Bible School to look after the East Arunachal Mission. It was through the untiring efforts of both Fr. George and Fr. Jose that today we have a huge population of Catholics in Arunachal Pradesh.

Fr. Jose picked up the language of the dominant Nyishi tribe (also known as Daflah) and started conducting mass in local dialects. He had great vision and started to build parish after parish in West Arunachal Pradesh. His relationship with the local leaders was amazing, and many senior politicians, as well as local IPS and IAS officers including those who had earlier persecuted Christians of Arunachal Pradesh, joined the Catholic faith. Clans like Nabom joined the church in great numbers. The former Chief Minister Nabom Tuki is an example of Fr. Jose's missionary maturity. On January 31, 1994, Fr. Jose, SDB, entered Itanagar to live and work with the people of West Arunachal Pradesh. He was the first priest to establish the parish of Itanagar for the Catholic Church. He lived and worked in a lowly thatched house. He tamed the Nyishi, the untamable ferocious warriors.

In 1993, when Fr. Kollandai (parish priest of West Arunachal Pradesh) left Harmurti Catholic Centre, there were about eight thousand Catholics in West Arunachal Pradesh, and when Fr. C. C. Jose left the state in 2004, there were more than eighty-five thousand Catholics (this number could be more than that of Manipur Archdiocese, which celebrated its Golden Jubilee in 2005). History and posterity will remember Fr. Kollandai as a man of great vision and fortitude.

Tadar Tanyang was a solid pillar for Fr. C. C. Jose while he was working with the Daflahs. He was the first Nyishi leader to be baptized into the Catholic Church by Rev. Bishop Kerketta at Dibrugarh on Holy Easter Sunday in 1979, in the presence of P. A. Sangma, former chief minister of Meghalaya and former speaker of the Indian Parliament; Ms. R. Shaiza, MP; H. S. Lyngdoh, former MP and former deputy chief minister of Meghalaya; G. S. Reddy, former MP; Bakin Pertin, former MP; and Archbishop Thomas Menamparampil. Tadar Tanyang desired to be baptized by only a bishop and chose Robert as his Christian name since Bishop Kerketta also has Robert as his first name. Tadar wanted that I should be his godfather. I was honored to be chosen as his godfather from among outstanding luminaries present during his baptism.

Fr. C. C. Jose, SDB, was loved by one and all, and, as a result, human as they are, many Catholic priests became jealous of him for his hard work. These priests began a whispering campaign against Fr. Jose in the West. The Holy Father appointed Fr. P. K. George, SDB as the bishop of Miao and Fr. John Thomas as the bishop of Itanagar.

I am absolutely shocked and worried about the future of the Church in Arunachal Pradesh. And sometime I question myself, "Have I made a Himalayan blunder?" But then I comfort myself thinking that priests, nuns, bishops, cardinals, and the Holy Father himself are after all human. The Chinese saying rings in my ears, "A little fragrance always clings to the hand that gives you roses."

The Catholic Church in Arunachal should take note of what happened to priests of *Vaishnavite* Hinduism of Bareghar Satra in Borduria, who alienated the subjects of the Nocte King. The church should have responsible priests with a vision to emulate Christ's teachings in letter and spirit. Lay leaders' advice should be heeded and not be taken as an intrusion.

The Nocte kings of Namsang and Borduria (they were brothers) had a very strong relationship with the Ahom king. They adopted the Bareghar Vaishnavite sect of Hinduism. However, worship was limited to the Nocte kings, and the kings' subjects were kept at bay from participating in the ritual worship of Hindu gods and goddesses.

When the Nocte Naga subjects came down from the hills to the plains to pay taxes and show obeisance to the high priest of Merbil, there was no warmth or bonding between the priest (teacher) and the devotee. The Nocte devotees were not allowed to participate in performing rituals of the satra. When the Nocte Naga went back after offering expensive *pujas* through the satra *goakhia* or the priest, the priest would sprinkle holy water to purify the places where the devotees had sat or slept. The devotees felt humiliated, and these purification ceremonies and religious exclusion were resented by the increasingly educated Nocte Naga tribal youth. Vaishnavism introduced the element of untouchability among the hill people, which was alien to their customs and beliefs. No tribe worth its name would tolerate such a system for long, and at an opportune time, they left Hinduism, and Hindu Vaishnavism slowly but surely disappeared from the Nocte society.

The establishment and blessing of the first Catholic Church of Arunachal Pradesh was truly a miracle. The way to the cross was definitely not an easy one, as described in the Bible—a narrow passage with plenty of pestilence, while on the left lay a broad road to evil.

■ ■ ■

Message of the Bishop of Dibrugarh[CE14]

BISHOP'S HOUSE
DIBRUGARH (ASSAM) INDIA
31ST JULY, 1979

Dearly Beloved Brethren,
    Sons and Daughters and
    People of Arunachal Pradesh

The Peace and grace of our Lord Jesus Christ be with you all. This is your Bishop speaking to you on the solemn occasion of the blessing of the newly built Church although he is not able to come personally to meet you due to the circumstances.

I send you my apostolic Blessing and I communicate to you the Blessing of the Holy Father, the Vicar of Christ and the successor of St. Peter. Although we are far away from each other we think of you, we pray for you and we love you. May God bless you, fill you with love and inspire you with courage. Be steadfast in Faith, constant in Hope and ardent in Charity.

Remember that our God is a God of love; our Religion is a Religion of love and the Law that God gave us is a Law of love. Therefore, love one another; help each other and pray for each other.

God has given you a new Church. It has been built with your hard labour and sacrifice. It is a gift of God. It is the House of God. It is a House of prayer. Therefore it is a holy place, though it may be humble. Therefore keep it sacred. Thank God for his gift. And pray for the Church, for the Holy Father; pray for the world and for our country and pray for our leaders so that God may give them wisdom to perform their duties with a sense of justice, righteousness and integrity. And finally pray for us too so that God may give us necessary help to carry on our work with zeal and love. May our heavenly Mother Mary help you and protect you in all your endeavours. Have courage! Christ is with you always. Christ Yesterday, Today and Forever.

Yours faithfully in C. J.
Robert Kerketta, SDB
Bishop of Dibrugarh

■ ■ ■

Saint Mother Teresa's visit to Borduria

Born in Skopje in Macedonia, Mother Teresa joined the Sisters of Loreto in Ireland at the age of 18 and after her training there she travelled to Calcutta to begin her missionary work amongst the poorest of the poor and the destitute. She established a new order called the Missionaries of Charity to look after people who no one was prepared to look after. She said, "Love cannot remain by itself, it has no meaning. Love has to be put into action, and that action is service". She came to be known as the 'Saint of the Gutters', a true missionary of charity, a mother of the poor and a symbol of compassion to the world. Her work gradually began to spread all over India and has a presence in over 130 countries now.

Despite her wish to visit Arunachal Pradesh and the numerous pleas made to the administration to obtain an inner line permit for her visit, permission was not granted by the state and central governments. However, after a lot of effort by us and with the support of the people and the Church, the administration finally capitulated and Mother Teresa was allowed to visit Arunachal Pradesh to inaugurate the Parish Church in Borduria and to lay the foundation stone for the Home of the Missionaries of Charity there. It was to be her first and only visit to the state.

Mother Teresa along with Archbishop Thomas Menamparampil, Bishop George Palliparambil, Sisters of the Missionaries of Charity, priests and nuns arrived in Borduria village on 2nd August 1993 (the same year that she received the Nobel Peace Prize) to bless the newly constructed 'pucca' church. Close to 5,000 people from Borduria and villages in the entire Tirap District attended the ceremonies. It was a historic moment for the state and further strengthened the presence of the Church in Arunachal Pradesh. After the solemn inauguration of the Parish Church, Mother Teresa, the church dignitaries, priests and nuns and the entire congregation were invited to my house for lunch. My mother Senphiak, wife Tei and my family worked through the night to cook the food and make all arrangements for the occasion. A special enclosure had been put up for seating Mother Teresa and the attending dignitaries, but the humble and down-to-earth Saint refused to sit there and went and sat down with the villagers to share food with them and interact with everyone present.

My mother Senphiak (now aged 96 years but still very active) has been a mother figure for all Christians in Borduria and her house was open to the nuns, religious brothers, priests, bishops, pastors and evangelists during the period of anti Christian policy of the government. Till 1989 there was no residential Christian institution to take care of the congregation and the church, hence many of them would spend a few nights while others would stay with her for months. She would lodge them and provide them simple food to eat. The small room where Mother Teresa stayed during her visit to Borduria was converted into a prayer and pilgrimage Centre on 1st August 2018 to celebrate the 25th anniversary of her visit. As a mark of appreciation, my mother Senphiak was given the honor to inaugurate the pilgrimage Centre at Borduria Church for her service during Mother Teresa's first and only visit to Arunachal Pradesh.

7

CONCLUSION

Religious persecution always involves a severe violation of the human right to religious freedom. The human right to religious freedom declares the moral and civic immunity of individuals and religious communities from coercion or violence on account of their religious beliefs and practice, which is guaranteed in the Universal Declaration of Human Rights and the United Nations Covenant on Civil and Political Rights.

Instead of following a policy of religious tolerance, administrators and political leaders in NEFA used the state machinery and enacted legislation in the form of the Arunachal Pradesh Freedom of Religion Act 1978 to actively persecute Christians and directly prevented people from converting to Christianity. Though the Bill provides only for prohibition of conversion by use of force or inducement or by fraudulent means, in actual practice, however, there was a systematic effort to block even the least Christian influence from penetrating the state, combined with an attempt to suppress the Christian community already in existence.

This is in direct contravention of the country's constitution and international legal conventions.

Mahatma Gandhi, the Father of our great nation, pointed out (in *Harijan* of September 9, 1935), "I believe that there is no such thing as conversion from one faith to another in the accepted sense of the word. It is a highly personal matter for the individual and his God." In another context, Gandhi even said, "I did once seriously think of embracing the Christian faith. The gentle figure of Christ, so full of forgiveness that he taught his followers not to retaliate when abused or struck, but to turn the other cheek—I thought it was a beautiful example of the perfect man."

The people of NEFA willingly embraced the Christian faith. There was no question of their being forced, induced, or fraudulently converted. They accepted Jesus as their savior on their own volition in the face of harassment, threats, physical torture, imprisonment, seizure and burning of Bibles, destruction of churches and property, denial of trade, commercial facilities and jobs, expulsion from society, and prohibition of construction of churches. All this has not deterred the people of Arunachal Pradesh from turning to Christ. There must be something extraordinary about Christ that He continues to draw people unto Him, in spite of all these hardships. It was a triumph of faith.

There is a tendency among some pastors and priests to follow the abiding wisdom of Shakespeare, "Do a little wrong to do a greater right." They must desist from following this proposition of Shakespeare at any cost if the Church is not to disintegrate. They must remember that had the mighty NEFA administration, with the tacit support of North Block, not persecuted the innocent early aborigine Christians of NEFA, systematically violating their human rights as well as their constitutional rights, the people of Arunachal Pradesh would have continued in the practice of animistic form of nature worship shining in their own genius.

I believe spirituality and religiosity are very precious and personal to all mankind. No one should insist on his or her fellow human beings to follow his religion. Respect all religions with malice toward none. Unfortunately, the shortsighted administrators had no vision and destroyed the fabric of the indigenous society by propagating a particular religion for the Arunachalee to follow. The administrator forgot that Hinduism too was foreign to the majority aborigines of NEFA (except for the Nocte tribe of Tirap district and Aka (or Hruso) and Miji tribes of West Kameng District).

The younger generation, enlightened with school and college education, soon realized that the propaganda of the state administration was wrong, and many of them joined Christian Churches. In the evolution of mankind, anything that is forced or bribed with inducement has its limitations, and people will ultimately rebel. The Ministry of Christ in Arunachal Pradesh grew from strength to strength on the shoulders of its dedicated and committed followers who stood up for their beliefs against all adversities and obstacles and succeeded in laying its unshakable foundation in the state.

Let our mistakes of the past enlighten us to serve humanity instead of forcing our views on the people forgetting the ancient Sanskrit saying "Aham Brahmasmi" (the core of my being is the ultimate reality, the root and ground of the universe, the source of all that exists). I hope the documentation about suppressing one religion and sponsoring another will throw some light on the "Rise of Christianity" in Arunachal Pradesh.

Albert Barnes rightly said, "It has become a settled principle that nothing which is good and true can be destroyed by persecution, but that the effect ultimately is to establish more firmly, and to spread more widely, that which it was designed to overthrow. It has long since passed into a proverb that 'the blood of the martyrs is the seed of the church.'"

ANNEXURE

1

IMPORTANT CHRISTIAN LEADERS OF ARUNACHAL PRADESH

Some of the important Christian leaders of Arunachal Pradesh are:

1. Late D. Ering, the first Union deputy minister in Jawaharlal Nehru's Ministry
2. Late Bakin Pertin, former MP
3. Late Jongpum Jugli, former MLA
4. Late Lokam Tado, former MLA
5. Late N. Ering, wife of late D. Ering
6. Rev. L. M. Yanger (also known as Langkhap Kimshing, the first Field Secretary among the Tangsa tribe)
7. Rev. Khoda Tana Tara (the first Field Secretary among the Nyishi tribe)
8. Late Tadar Tanyang, former minister
9. Late Oken Lego, former MLA
10. Rev. Osik Pertin
11. Toko Chilee

12. Toko Kach
13. Late Tiggalon Borang, Rtd. DC
14. Late Tingpong Wangham, former minister
15. Late Ranlam Dada
16. Late Rev. Yontam Lego
17. Daniel Teli
18. Tapom Jamoh, former MLA
19. Martin Dai, former chief secretary of Arunachal Pradesh
20. Neelam Taram, former home minister
21. Rev. Likha Dodum (first deacon appointed from the Nyishi tribe)
22. Tero Kakho (first catechist of Arunachal Pradesh)
23. Sister Nygan Medam, MC (first nun of Arunachal Pradesh)
24. Rev. Anggon Ratan
25. Dr. B. Tada
26. Boa Tamo, former MLA
27. Chamai Rajkumari (Princess of the Namsang royal family)
28. Jati Pulu, former member APSC
29. Former CS
30. Kimi Aya, IPS
31. Komlang Mosang, minister
32. L. Wanglat, former home and finance minister
33. Late N. Natung, former minister
34. Nabam Tuki, former chief minister
35. Rev. Molam Rongrang
36. Late Setong Sena, former minister
37. T. T. Gamdik, IAS
38. Takam Sanjoy, MP
39. Thangwang Wangham, former minister
40. Wangdung Lowangcha
41. Late Wanglam Sawin, MLA

42. Y. D. Perme, Rtd. IAS
43. Rev. T. Lama
44. Biamin Mosang
45. Bita Kumar Sena, former APPCS
46. Late Chagan Medam
47. Rev. Chingkha Chippo
48. Christine Wanglat, Dy. Director
49. D. S. Solu, IRS
50. Duwang Matey
51. Gaberal Wangsu, MLA
52. Gamdik, IAS
53. Hage Khoda, IAS
54. Late Hangkang Dada
55. Hibu Tamang, IPS
56. James Tachi, former president of Nyishi Baptist Council
57. Rev. John Borang
58. Rev. Fr. John from Along
59. Kameng Dollo, former deputy chief minister
60. Kamki, Secretary
61. Kamthok Lowang, former MLA
62. Kapa Kholie, IAS
63. Lekha Saya, MLA
64. Rev. Likha Ama
65. Pastor Manwang Lowang
66. Michi Paku, IPS
67. Nido Pavitra, former Parliamentary Secretary
68. Nik Kamen, MLA
69. Rev. Mikam Perme
70. P. Hosai, Rtd. Additional Resident Commissioner
71. T. L. Rajkumar, former speaker and minister for twenty years

72. Tabom Tasar
73. Rev. Tanya Riram
74. Rev. Tar Choya
75. Rev. Ter Tana
76. Wanglin Lowangdong, chief of Borduria and MLA
77. Wangton Lowang, Asst. Director
78. Yumsen Matey, former MLA

2

BORDURIA CHURCH BUILDERS

The following clan leaders and supporters were the people who helped me build the church in Borduria without asking for any remuneration. Moreover, all of them were not Christians at the time of construction of the church:

    Atom Tangjang
    Late Chagan L. Medam
    Late Chanlang Moanchan
    Late Chinjam Poantey
    Late Dohwang L. Medam
    Duwang Matey
    Late Ganchan Lamra
    Late Gawang L. Medam
    Late Hangkang Dadam
    Late Hangtan Dadam
    Late Hapan Ruttum
    Late Hawang Lowang
    Hiannyak Henkhe

Late Hoankam Poantey
Late Janpi Khetey
Kamwang L. Medam
Late Kelow Poantey
Late Khampe L. Medam
Khampong Matey
Late Khelang Khetey
Late Khoawang Tocchu
Kupong Lamra
Late Lohpong Dadam
Late Lohwang Henkhe
Late Longam Wangha
Late Lopong Dadam
Minjah Lama
Moangkhiak Moanwang
Late Nahang Ruttum
Late Nahwang Tangdong
Late Ngoanphiak Mongchan
Late Noapwang Medam
Late Nokrian Matey
Noksen Lama
Late Nokpong Ruttum
Late Phangwang L. Medam
Late Phoajah Wangha
Late Phoane Homchha
Late Phoaren Matey
Ramlang Khetey
Ranjian Tangjang
Ranlang Lama
Rantung Lamra
Late Sanwang Dadam

Somtung Lamra
Late Summat Ruttum
Teboam Matey
Late Techan Ruttum
Late Teche Mema
Late Tedan Khetey
Late Teko Moanchan
Late Tejan Matey
Tejit Matey
Tenok Lokkhow
Late Tephoa Ruttum
Late Teram Khetey
Late Tesun Matey
Late Tetang Ruttum
Late Tethiam Dadam
Thinhak Dadam
Late Thinnyak Matey
Late Wahoang Mongchan
Wakha Lowang
Waku Matey
Late Wangchan Longkarian
Wangdo Lama
Late Wangdoan Lamra
Wangjut H. Lowang
Late Wangkhoan L. Medam
Late Wanglap Ruttum
Wanglee Lowangchaa
Late Wangloa Ruttum
Wangman Lowangchaa
Wangmat Lokkhow
Late Wangngam L. Medam

Late Wangnoam Lowang
Late. Wangnoan Dadam
Late Wangnoap Matey
Late Wangphoa L. Medam
Wangsun Lowang
Wangtang L. Medam
Late Wangtoan H. Lowang
Late Wapoan Matey
Late Watho Tangjang

3

BAPTISM OF CATHOLICS—
IMPORTANT DATES

August 15, 1976: Tero Kakho from Kamai village was baptized, who later became a full-time catechist.

August 6, 1978: L. Wanglat and his family became the first Catholic family of Arunachal Pradesh. However, there are numerous claims by individuals among the Apatani that some of them had taken baptism into the Catholic Church in the early 1970s. To substantiate these claims, we do not have any records from either the lay activists or the church. It is interesting to note that not a single Apatani Catholic came forward to meet the Christian MP delegation that visited Zero in 1978. It is quite possible that some adventurous Apatani youth might have taken baptism from the North Lakhimpur parish. However, those baptized in the early days by Catholic priests in Assam felt it prudent to lie low after seeing the atrocities inflicted on the Nyishi, by government-sponsored prosecutors. It was not until Modan Laling along with Gyati Taka, Boa Tamo, Lokam Tado, and Tadar

Tanyang began to participate as Catholic laity from 1977 to 1978 that Catholic Christians came out into the open to profess their faith.

1979: Around seventy Noctes were baptized at different times.

July 16–30, 1979: This was the period of the ongoing fight for Inner Line Permit for the team of religious leaders for the blessing of the Church with DC of Tirap as well as the Government of Arunachal and the people of Borduria. (On seeing the great struggle faced by the people of Borduria, neighboring clan leaders insisted on being baptized on the same day as the blessing of the Church!).

August 1, 1979: The team of religious authorities arrived in Borduria.

August 2, 1979: Blessing of the Church at Borduria. Bishop Kerketta, SDB, along with six other priests openly baptized 776 souls on the soil of Arunachal Pradesh, braving persecution and arrest under the Arunachal Pradesh Freedom of Religion Act. Before the baptism actually took place, the bishop of Dibrugarh announced that those who really wanted to be baptized should come forward and that if anyone took baptism under any sort of compulsion the baptism was not valid.

4

CHRISTIAN CHRONICLES OF ARUNACHAL PRADESH IN BRIEF

1840: Rev. Miles Bronson works in Namsang Village, Tirap District

1851–54: Fr. Nicolas Michael Krick works among the Adis and Mishmis

1854: Fr. Krick and Fr. Augustine Etienne Bourry die for their faith at Somme village beyond the Mishmi area

1945: Regulation forbidding Arunachal tribals to use the services of a lawyer without the Political Officer's permission

1953: Union Cabinet decision to ban the entry of Christianity into Arunachal Pradesh

1969: Churches in the villages of Dem, Deed and Neelam of Subansiri District are burnt down on Government orders

1969: Intimidation of Christians in the villages of Kjamlang and Karsang

1970: Arrest of Dikang Murang, Samman Murang and Yonglim Taikam for being Christians

1970: Externment order given to Tai Christians of Dipa Village who were compelled to put their thumb impression on a statement renouncing Christianity

1970: Churches in villages of Magi, Dipa and Dipoo of Siang District burnt down

1971: Churches in the villages of Kih, Peri, Thaw, Apoo of Subansiri District burnt down

1974: Death of Tana Ekha of Sango village as a result of torture. Churches in the following villages burnt down: Khemli, Naharlagun, Laptap, Revi, Pang, Yalling, Sacho, Karoi, Gotupo, Bogia, Lidhi, Tabi, Gai, Khil, Lakhil, Legan, Genga, Pacho, Depo, Grammaopop, Leru, Balijan, Cher and Pick

1974: Teli Ekhu, wife of Teli Tad of Khemti village, stripped naked in public and hung upside down

1974: More than 60 Christian houses burnt down with 150 houses destroyed on the order of Arunachal Pradesh Government

1975: Tadar Tang asks the Christians of Nyishi tribe in a reconciliation meeting in the presence of K. A. A. Raja, Bishop

Chryssotom, Bishop D. D. Pradhan, A. Kisku, MP and others to renounce their faith

1978: The Legislative Assembly in Arunachal passes the Arunachal Pradesh Freedom of Religion Bill. Later it receives the President's assent in spite of the protests from all over the country

1978: Techi Takar, Minister of Animal Husbandry sends a blasphemous memorandum to the President of India. He also writes to the Executive Engineer to bar Christians from getting contract assignments

1978: The people of Lekhi, Genga and other villages spend their Christmas in jungles

1979: Hapjong Jugli and two other Christians are arrested under Section 3 of the Arunachal Pradesh Freedom of Religion Act and kept in prison for 30 days without a charge sheet being given to them

1979: Christians of Salang village take down their Church under threat of imprisonment and torture

1980: Ashok Kumar, DC, Khonsa, Tirap issues a circular, vide order No. CA 128/79 dt. 12.6.80 forbidding construction of places of worship. Anyone found violating his order are to be prosecuted

1980: In the month of April, 12 persons from Nokfan village are arrested for converting to Christianity—Wanglam Tikam, Waktum Wangsu, Ranku Apesam, Ngompha Wangsu, Mandum Apesam, Wangto Wangsu, Manto Wangsu, Wangman Wangsu,

Mokdum Wangsu, Nokkam Wangsu, Honga Wangsu and Hondon Wangsu, Lokha. These innocent youths are convicted by ADC, Khonsa (Class I Magistrate) on 24th January 1980 under the Arunachal Pradesh Freedom of Religion Act 1978 for accepting Christ as their personal saviour. They are ordered to pay a fine of Rs. 2,000 each

15th July 1980: Gegong Apang, Chief Minister, participating in the inaugural session of North-Eastern State Hills Congress (I) meeting states that "Christian missionaries with the help of new converts are trying to bring instability in the state." Therefore Christian missionaries will not be allowed in Arunachal Pradesh

1981: Inner Line Permit refused to the Bishop of Dibrugarh for celebrating Christmas with the Christians of Borduria. He had applied for a permit for 3 days only

1981: Advocate M. A. Rahman, Advocate Ekka, Senior Advocate Anil Kaunda and Senior Advocate Choudhary, appointed to defend Christians of Borduria, Nokfan, Lathong, Longo and Moktow villages, accused under Freedom of Religion Act 1978

1981: Moktow village Church burnt down under government order. T. L. Rajkumar, Speaker was the person who helped to burn down the Church; we have indisputable facts to prove his active involvement

1983: G. B. of Perakat village is ordered to submit a list of persons who have embraced Christianity to Circle Officer of Bordumsa for appropriate penal action vide his confidential letter No. CON. 9/83/444-45 of 21.3.83

1986: DC, Khonsa refuses to register the Christian Organization "The Christian Association of Tirap" under the Societies Act. This Association is affiliated to AICU (All India Catholic Union)

25th April 1987: The following persons are arrested U/S IPC 294A: L. N. Wanglat, Tingpong Wangham, T. Homcha, Wanglom Homcha, Rangkap Matey, Mossang, Wangthian Hakhun, Mandun Apesam and Namchai Wangsa. Their crime was that these persons collected some donations for the 1986 Christmas celebrations from their well wishers and fellow Christians. The total collection was a mere Rs. 4,000 and this amount was donated by Christians only through the Missionaries of Charity Brothers

4th June 1987: Brother Anand and Brother Das of Mother Teresa's Missionaries of Charity who were working with Christian Association of Tirap District were arrested and deported in the dead of the night from Borduria village vide order No. 52/87-1 of 4.6.87 passed by 1st Class Magistrate A. Bhattacharjee of Khonsa

20th October 1887: Wangkum Ronrang, Pastor arrested by Circle Officer, Manmao vide his order No. MOC-7-86-87/391-93 of 20.10.87 to stop preaching and baptizing immediately and he is to take permission for moving around in his own parish

1987: Circle Officer, Pumao orders Christian people of Bomia village to participate and worship with those practicing the animist occult faith, failing which they are to pay Rs. 1,000 each

1987: Niausa Church completely destroyed on the instruction of DC, Tirap

1987: Nokgan Wangpan, a Pastor from Bonia village is arrested by SP, Tirap on a fictitious allegation

1987: Noklai Wangsu of Pamao village is arrested by B. B. Rai, Extra Assistant Commissioner, Longding and kept in a lockup for one month for taking baptism from Pastor Wangpan

1987: Inner Line Permit is refused by the Addl. Deputy Commissioner G. S. Pillai, vide letter No. IL-5/87/PI-II of 23.12.87 to Bishop of Dibrugarh and his party for visiting Borduria for three days to celebrate Christmas with the Christians of Borduria

1988: On 11.3.88 Molem Ronrang, Pastor cum TBCC secretary is ordered by Circle Officer, Manmao vide letter No. MOC-7/86/1015 dt. 11.3.88 to stop preaching, failing which serious action would be taken against him

1988: Pulai Wangpan and Pongbo Wangsu, Catechist of Longphong village are arrested on false and trumped up charges. They were released after 7 months in solitary confinement for want of evidence

1988: Arunachal Police hunts for M. Wangsu, Pastor of Chopsa village, for preaching and baptizing

1988: Wangian Wangsu and five others arrested from Ninu village for accepting Christianity. They were released on bail of Rs. 10,000 each. The case is still pending in DC, Tirap's Court. Advocate Bipin Gohain is defending the case

1986–1988: No Priest or Pastor is allowed to come for celebrating Christmas

26th December 1988: The Church in Along, Head Quarters of Siang District is destroyed under the supervision of Dagi Bagra, Class II Magistrate (Circle Officer)

1989: The Church in Kayeng village is destroyed with the help of the local Government

1989: On the atrocities meted out to churches in Arunachal Pradesh, Bakin Partin, MLA raises the issue with the Speaker in the last Assembly. His views are neither accepted nor recorded in the Assembly proceedings

We challenge any one disputing persecution of Christians in Arunachal Pradesh. Those who speak of upholding secularism should ensure that Christians in Arunachal should be allowed to have schools, hospitals and missionaries to work with Arunachal Christians

*The above chronicle was published by the Chairman and Secretary of Arunachal Christian Action Committee, Mission Compound, TBCC, P. O. Lakla, Jagun, Via Ledo, Assam.

5

ARTICLES ON PERSECUTION OF CHRISTIANS IN ARUNACHAL PRADESH

The following articles were published by me as the Chairman of Arunachal Christian Action Committee in 1980 titled "Isolation is the solution for persecution of Christians in Arunachal Pradesh." I am including these articles to highlight the historical movement by a few and dedicated secular leaders in the midst of persecution by the then administrators, political leadership, panchayat officials, student unions, and village authorities as per the 1945 regulation. These institutions were encouraged and funded by the government of the day to persecute the 1% Christians of Arunachal Pradesh. Had there not been mindless persecution against Christians in the late 1960s, 1970s, 1980s, and as late as 1999 maybe the Christian population would not have been as it is now. Now the indigenous Christian population in the state of Arunachal Pradesh is estimated to be above 50 percent.

■ ■ ■

On March 27, 1979, the Union Home Minister H. M. Patel stated on the floor of the Lok Sabha that there was no harassment of Christians in Arunachal Pradesh. He called the allegations of large scale destruction of churches a "fantastic nonsense."

We want to tell you that what has been described as "fantastic nonsense" is a historic fact, and that what has been flatly denied actually took place. I further want to tell you that neither the demolition of individual churches, nor harassment of individual Christians, was an administrative lapse due to some overzealous officer, but a part of an overall strategy for throttling the young Christian community in Arunachal Pradesh, a strategy formulated sometime after Independence and firmly adhered to by successive administrators during the last two decades.

■ ■ ■

Kutcha Church

H. M. Patel, Union Home Minister, reluctantly admitted that a *"kutcha church"* was demolished by some people who had gone back from their Christian faith to their original tribal beliefs.

Why a *"kutcha church"*? Because Christians were not permitted to construct *"pucca"* (permanent RCC buildings) churches in Arunachal Pradesh for a period of 50 years from 1950 to 2000[CE16] . Subsequently, as Christianity grew in spite of persecution from the then government, RCC church buildings were constructed by the local indigenous tribes of Arunachal Pradesh, daring the government to take action against them.

In fact, the erection of any type of place of worship is forbidden in the state, except those that belong to the indigenous faith. (However, Hindu and Buddhist temples are being built anyway under the name of some tribal deity, e.g. at Along, Khonsa,

Deomali, Ziro, Tezu, Bomdila, etc., though the local people resent it.)

If you ask for permission to build a church, yours is an unauthorized construction and you will be given demolition orders. You may challenge the authorities for a while and continue for some time, but systematic harassment begins. You may be given an externment order. You may not be tolerated even in the deep jungles.

If any of your relatives are government servants, they will be threatened with demotion, transfer and dismissal on flimsy grounds. If you are holding a business license, it may be taken away. If your children are enjoying government stipends, these could be cut off. If there is a dissenting group in the village, they are bribed to do the demolition work for the administration. Or else, you may be threatened with imprisonment and torture, until you think it wiser to take down the thatch-roofed church for mere survival.

■ ■ ■

Sentiments of the Tribal People

Subsequently, H. M. Patel claimed that it was in consideration for the sentiments of the tribal people that the erection of churches was not allowed. The contrary is the truth.

Permission was refused even when the majority of the people of a village (and in some cases all) were Christians. Let us take the example of the Songking Village Church in the then Tirap District. All the villagers were Christians, nobody's peace was disturbed, but a demolition order came in spite of that. If there was any consideration for the sentiments of the tribal people, the administration could not have done that.

The tribal people in Northeast India are extremely tolerant in matters of religion. They are the last people to object if any one of their fellow villagers accepts a new religion. It is very common to see in the same family members belonging to different religious persuasions. Such a thing would be unthinkable in most other parts of India. The usual reply you receive from parents, friends, and relatives on matters of religion is "it is up to him or her." Each one decides for oneself which religion suits him or her. In such a society it is not easy for anyone to accept that fellow villagers will burn down a church without bribes and threats and active encouragement from someone else. And that someone else has always been a man from the administration. Evidences are too many to allow any further doubt on the matter.

The demolition of churches has hurt the sentiments of two sets of tribal people, the Christians who lost their places of worship, and the people who demolished them because they were compelled to act against their convictions. Complete disrespect was shown to the sentiments of the tribal people by this act.

■ ■ ■

Tribals Who Reconverted to Their Original Faiths

H. M. Patel said that a church was demolished by some Christians who reconverted themselves to their original faith.

The real story is different. It is not that the people went back to their original faith on their own. They were compelled to renounce Christianity. There have been too many instances of compulsion used for extorting a formal renunciation of the Christian faith. Christian applicants for jobs are told that there is no work for them unless they place a thumb impression on a document renouncing Christianity. The same thing is done for Christians applying for licenses or seeking government contracts and with villagers who are easily bullied. Often a village council (Kebang, Nguangtun, etc.) is called together on the initiative of the Circle Officer or the Extra Assistant Commissioner and the Christian is made to denounce Christianity in public or be penalized. Those who thus cooperate with the Government are rewarded. Mysteriously, teachers, bus drivers, and the most petty officers have abrogated to themselves powers for which they found official encouragement in their anti-Christian activities. According to reports, the then Lieutenant Governor's discretionary funds have been made available for such anti-Christian activities.

In case of Salang village (referred to by H. M. Patel), the threat of imprisonment and torture was used to compel the people to renounce (at least extremely) Christianity and take down their church. Immediately before the demolition incident, three Christians had been arrested under Section 3 of the Arunachal Pradesh Freedom of Religion Act, as a salutary warning to the villagers. H. M. Patel would have done well to tell the Lok Sabha who had master-minded the reconversion of Christians into their traditional beliefs.

■ ■ ■

Demolition of Churches

The demolition of a small church in Salang village is certainly not an isolated case. The number of demolition orders from the District Commissioners and the Circle Officers in my files are so many as to establish beyond any doubt that the demolition of churches is a part of the standing policy of the Government of Arunachal Pradesh. Not a single document sanctioning the construction of a church is in existence, while we have any number of written threats, warnings, and actual orders for demolition of churches. Are we then to accept that the demolition of the church at Salang village was a lone incident and that it was done by the people themselves on their own?

During the last two and half decades more than 100 churches in Arunachal Pradesh were destroyed at the government's instigation. No amount of denial will nullify the fact. In the case of Arunachal, the traditional solution has always been the same: flatly deny everything. Sometimes the government would take one bold step further: institute an enquiry to be conducted under the auspices of the guilty party itself!

■ ■ ■

Destruction of Christian Homes

It has been the mania of the administration to harass the Christian community by setting their houses on fire. Accidents can be caused! Disasters can be pre-arranged, and there are always willing accomplices, especially when the remuneration is very tempting.

There are thousands of witnesses to general destruction of Christian property since 1974. Christian homes and granaries were put to fire, domestic animals robbed and their household goods taken away. Christians had to live in the jungles for months. They were told to get out of Arunachal Pradesh and to go to a "Christian" state like Nagaland, Meghalaya or Mizoram. Several fled to Assam and lived there as refugees. The Arunachal authorities refused to provide relief for the sufferers. Medicines and rations were denied to them because they were Christians. There are so many Christians who have witnessed such incidents that the very denial of harassment of Christians in Arunachal Pradesh is a "fantastic nonsense."

Christians have got so used to hardships over the years, that they do not even know how to describe their woes. Even the educated man today has been brought up under the dictatorship of the administration. Democracy never functioned in the Union Territory. The first elections took place 30 years after Independence and the administration heckled the opposition. In such a situation, it has been very difficult even for the educated men to receive their education outside the Union Territory. Shillong was considered particularly dangerous for its Christian influence. The more enlightened and liberal-minded sections of the people are just beginning to organize themselves and make their voices heard. The ruling group in the 70s, 80s and 90s were quite unused to the ways of democracy and was surprised that anyone should speak up and differ from them.

■ ■ ■

Story Behind the Demolition

The harassment of Christians, which had been going on for a long time, took on a new dimension after the passing of the Arunachal Pradesh Freedom of Religion Bill in 1978. The officers and agents of the Government acquired new confidence.

On February 21, 1979, Hapjong Jugli of Kantang village was arrested under section 3 of the Arunachal Pradesh Freedom of Religion Act along with Tukhim Jugli and Hangkham Jugli. Bail was promised, but not given. No charge-sheet was issued. (This has been the usual procedure in Arunachal Pradesh.) They were kept in prison for 30 days without trial. They were told that they would be set free if they renounced Christianity. After a month in prison, Tukhim Jugli and Hangkham Jugli were taken out of the prison and asked whether they would like to remain in prison for a life time or sign a document renouncing Christianity.

Much against their will, the two broken men agreed to sign the document.

Then Hapjong Jugli was taken out of prison and told how the others had adopted a reasonable attitude. He was also pressurized into signing a similar document, which he did most reluctantly. We have this information through a secret letter we received from him written on 25.3.1979 from Kantang village where he is practically under house-arrest and from where he managed to smuggle out his message.

We must keep this background in mind when we speak of the demolition story. Salang is a small village with a population of about 100 people, half of whom became Christians a year ago. It is true that the non-converted tribal people resented the decision of their fellow villagers, but they were made to resent by means of threats, warnings and false propaganda.

It is very easy to understand how the administration, that is the absolute master in the interior regions of Arunachal Pradesh, can get anything done. People were told that if they did not give up Christianity, they would all be put in prison as some of their fellow Christians had been. You need to know the psychology of these villagers who are at the mercy of the Administrator and who can appeal only to the same administration's machinery for justice.

They have never gone out of the Arunachal Pradesh. No outsider has come to them during the last 30 years except those who have been carefully screened by the administration. They know nothing of legal procedures. (Incidentally, legal procedures do not exist in Arunachal Pradesh, at least in the way we know them). A 1945 regulation that still holds well says that an Arunachal Pradesh tribal cannot even use a lawyer's services without the D. C.'s permission. That in the twentieth century!

Thus the people of Salang village were compelled to take down their church for mere survival. Union Home Minister H. M. Patel was, in a way, right!

■ ■ ■

The Untold Tale of Arunachal Pradesh
The Christian Community in India has recently been much worried about happenings in Arunachal Pradesh, and rightly because unspeakable things have happened in this part of the country.

First of all, when you speak of the Christian community in Arunachal Pradesh, think of simple villagers who do not know how to defend their rights in public forums and in law courts (there were nothing like legal processes in Arunachal Pradesh). Think of a group that had become outcasts in a casteless society during the same period.

The few Christian young men who have been to school and the fewer who have been to college are just beginning to make their voices heard, but they need the support of their co-religionists in other parts of the country so that their voices may not be a cry in the wilderness. One thing worthwhile the young church has done is that it has kept an accurate chronicle (not complete to be sure) of recent persecution. One day the account will be published.

■ ■ ■

Weeding Out Christianity
The administration felt it their sacred and bounden duty to weed out the dangerous creeper that was stretching its wild shoots into the high Himalayas: Christianity. Even before

Independence there was a small community of Christians in Arunachal Pradesh. In spite of persecution, the Christian community registered a steady growth. No missionary (not even Indian) ever worked in NEFA. The preachers of Christianity were all local men and women who had fallen deeply in love with Christ. And the religion of Christ spread from man to man, from home to home.

When the Administrator raises a hue and cry about "foreign" influence in Arunachal Pradesh or a CIA hand, it makes no sense at all to anyone who knows anything about the actual situation in our state. Not to speak of foreign, not even Indian Christian preachers are allowed into NEFA. In 1978, a priest who had gone to meet his friends in Tirap district with a regular permit valid for two weeks (a unique case in 30 years), was given a quit order by the D. C., Tirap within 24 hours, though, having been involved in an accident, the priest was lying in a hospital bed in Dibrugarh. And what is more interesting, soon after that the D. C. was given a promotion (for such admirable vigilance!).

The Christian community in Arunachal grew not due to any help it received from outside, but in spite of the absence of it. There was no Christian inducement to speak of; all the inducement was on the other side. Anyone who gave up Christianity, or offered to persecute the Christians, was given suitable remuneration by the Administration. Would-be Christians of Arunachal Pradesh went to Assam, Meghalaya and Nagaland begging for baptism, pleading for Bibles, eagerly asking for Christian literature. Could a Christian heart refuse? With the spiritual food that these means provided, the Christian community in the state kept alive and grew in strength.

The Administration watched with alarm the amazing growth of the Christians. Every stratagem was devised to restrict growth of the Christian community within a particular area, to prevent further growth, and root it out wherever possible. When everything failed they took up arms in active persecution.

■ ■ ■

What the Christians Ask For

The Christians in Arunachal Pradesh are willing to forget the past and forgive the present as long as they are guaranteed a peaceful future. They cannot afford to keep silent with the possibility that a worse persecution may break out at any time. Preparations are going on, threats continue, stray incidents take place all the time, and crime has become legal with the passing of an unconstitutional bill. Christian students get no scholarships, Christian young men no jobs.

They ask for nothing except for those rights guaranteed by the Constitution. They want that the Christian community in Arunachal Pradesh should have the liberty of belief, faith and worship as guaranteed by the Preamble to the Constitution.

They want that the Christian community in Arunachal Pradesh should not suffer any discrimination only on grounds of religion (Article 15.1 Indian Constitution).

They want that the Christian community in Arunachal Pradesh should be given freedom of conscience and the right freely to profess, practice and propagate religion (Article 25.1 Indian Constitution).

They want that the Christian community in Arunachal Pradesh should be given the freedom to establish and administer educational institutions of their own choice (Article 30.1 Indian Constitution).

They want nothing more, they will accept nothing less!!

■ ■ ■

Did Christian Missionaries Detribalize the North-East?

The Christian missionary has been accused of detribalizing tribal people. Verrier Elwin's chief complaint was that the missionaries destroy "their art, their dances, their weaving and their whole culture." But with all his wide acquaintance with tribal matters he could adduce only one example of an unhappy Christian missionary measure which had been conceived in the last century when the entire philosophy of the civilized man's dealings with tribal people was still "primitive" in any part of the world.

We know for certain that "later day missionaries sensibly tried to preserve all that was good in old tradition" (Robert Reid). It may even be that whatever of tribal art and culture will survive, will survive only due to the untiring efforts of Christian institutions and Christian missionaries. When speaking of detribalization it is important to remember that in every tribal area the Administration was the first to enter. "To set the record straight, it is necessary to assert that it was not the church which entered the hills first. The first to enter the difficult terrain was the administration" (Shibanikinkar Chaube). Then came often enough the people whom Elwin abhorred most: "merchants, money-lenders, landlords and liquor vendors." Where they could not penetrate in person, they controlled from outside. It is well known how much of tribal economy is in the hands of the non-tribals. When Christianity first entered the scene, the detribalization process had long been ruining the tribal society.

The detribalization process we are speaking of is too complex to allow simple answers. Enough studies have been conducted on the detribalization of tribal societies throughout the world to convince us that no single agency having dealings with the tribals can afford to throw stones at another, least of all the administration. Take the case of Arunachal Pradesh. The policy of the administration was phrased by Elwin thus: "We wish to see that they have better houses, a higher yield for their labour in the fields, improved techniques for their home industries" *(A Philosophy of NEFA)*. Excellent! But admit that detribalization has begun. An outside agent, however benevolent, has entered. A. Malinowsky says, "Culture is an originally integrated whole." Elements of culture are so inter-knit that you cannot tamper with one without running the risk of metamorphosing the entire organism.

Lauriston Sharp makes an interesting study of the social revolution caused among the Yir Yoront tribals of Australia by the mere introduction of the steel age in the place of the stone axe they had. The stone axes had played such a key role in their culture that, with the coming of its cheaper and easily available substitute, the whole economy, social and family relations and even religious life of the Yir Yoront tribe were thrown out of gear. "Human culture is constituted of various aspects which are not isolated but form an organic whole. A change in one aspect reverberates in others" (R. N. Haldipur). For example, the state, district and sub-divisional authorities weaken traditional leadership in a village which was a self-contained whole, money economy destroys the barter system and accentuates inequality, modern education kills the *Morung* (bachelors' dormitory) training and village discipline. What then, is the solution to the tribal problem? Isolation? The monopoly rule of the Administration? Or, the freedom guaranteed by the Constitution?

■ ■ ■

Christians Are Accused of Bringing in "Westernization"
Christianity is said to have westernized the tribals of Northeast India. Now, we would like to ask what the meaning of westernization is. Have you studied its causes, its processes, its stages, its consequences? When is a person westernized?

Was Russia westernized when Peter the Great reshaped the government machinery after the French fashion, or when he introduced the Prussian type of military organization, or when he asked men to cut their beards and smoke profusely? Was Japan westernized when that country borrowed western political notions, western industry, or adopted western dress? Were the Turks western when they put on the hat, and the Nigerians when they went to the pools, or the Hawaiians when they listened to the Beatles? Have Indians been westernized because they have adopted western democratic institutions or the Philippinos because they keep Christmas or the Malays because they wear trousers? Is one westernized when he eats bread and butter, or uses spoons and forks or speaks English?

Have the Japanese remained true to their original identity despite the industrial revolution, and the Philippinos after adopting Christianity and the Indians after imbibing western political and social notions? If they have, can the tribals not remain true to themselves after adopting whatever elements of the western culture they think suitable? If they have not, why such excitement about the tribals alone "becoming westernized"?

What is essential to western culture? Efficiency? Punctuality? Organization? Planning? Nuclear Family? What is essential to

Indian culture? Opposite of all these? Hospitality? Spirituality? A philosophic attitude to life? What is essential to culture, values or forms? If forms, which forms? There are no easy answers.

If someone says that the tribal Christian is westernized, he is making a very bold statement. He should be specific. Is he any more westernized than the people in the other parts of the country, more than his non-tribal brethren? The tribal Christian eats the same food, lives in the same type of house, works in the same type of fields as people do in the other parts of India, allowing for the local and tribal variations. He keeps his village festivities, and goes about his daily round of life like co-villagers. Women retain their traditional dress, and most men dress themselves in their traditional outfit. Of course, the urban population and those that have been to school usually prefer to wear trousers and build pucca houses and use English and have a transistor radio. But the same thing happens all over India among the educated and urbanized people. Still someone will say there are perversions in western culture some of which have been adopted.

If that is true, it is equally true that the Christian church has consistently stood against them. The church has always taught that what is not worthy of man is not for Christians. But then let us not forget that every culture has its own weaknesses. Thus the Indian society has taken some of its diseases to the tribals as well: the slum, the beggar-institution, the caste system with its side effects like inferiority-superiority complexes and social barriers. Such things were unknown to tribal society. We wish that steps were taken to control these diseases too.

A casual and spontaneous remark made by Asoso Yonuo, a Naga writer, in his book *The Rising Nagas* is extremely revealing. He says, "Yet, it can be said that Christianity succeeded in winning converts because of the fact that apart from Biblical stories, the teachings of Christianity and western social life and ethics were identical to the animistic beliefs and social life of the Garos, Khasis, Mizos and Nagas." Asoso is not enthusiastic for Christianity by any means. He is only explaining. The idea contained in this statement, if sufficiently studied, may give us the key to the relationship between the tribal and western culture. Experts tell us, for instance, that the music of certain tribes is closer to western than to Indian music.

What Asoso says is confirmed by the conduct of the Arunachal elite. They were brought up in a hot house atmosphere and exposed to "Indian culture" (by which the Administration means Hindu culture) and carefully guarded from "western culture" (by which is meant any Christian influence). And yet when they come out to meet their tribal brethren in other parts of North-East India, they reveal the same tribal character, attitudes to life, likes and dislikes and code of conduct. Who westernized them?

But the fundamental question is, is an individual or society not free to choose the food they will eat, the dress they will wear, the feasts they will keep, the language they will speak, the script they will use? Or is the anthropologist-administrator going to tell them what to wear because his ancestors were more lightly clad? All our ancestors had styles and habits that no one seems eager to revive. The ancient Angles, Saxons, Celts, Franks, and Slavs had institutions, costumes, arts and other glories that are now recorded only in books of history, or preserved in museums. A stage comes for every people to decide for themselves how they want to shape their future. Grant them that freedom!

The most serious accusation is that the Christians are responsible for all the troubles in North-East India. We would like to ask who were responsible for the extreme groups among the Meiteis, for the demand for statehood of the Ahoms and the demand for the Roman script by the Bodos, all of whom are Hindus.

M. N. Srinivas and R. D. Sanwal say, "Blaming the 'rebelliousness', 'inherent separation', or similar 'ills' of the NEHA (North Eastern Hill Areas) tribes upon such favourite whipping horses as the 'legacy of colonialism', 'conservation of the tribes', 'ethnic myopia', or 'activities of foreign missionaries', only helps in diverting attention from identifying the real factors responsible for weak integration."

In a seminar convened by the Indian Institute of Advanced Study, Shimla, in 1969, Ms. Terhuja from Nagaland argued eloquently, "It is no use blaming Christian missionaries. The persistent accusation of foreign missionaries as fomenting the present trouble betrays our lack of understanding of our own affairs."

Tribal grievances are manifold. The first sore point, everywhere in tribal areas, is loss of tribal land. Elwin says, "Thus the Kol insurrection of 1833 was caused by encroachment on tribal land. The Tanar rebellions, repeated seven times between 1789 and 1832, were primarily due to the illegal deprivation of their rights in land which the Hos, Mundas, and Uraons had suffered. Anxiety about land or the active exploitation of it by outsiders had led to many other disturbances such as the Rampa rebellion in East Godavari, the Bastar rising of 1911, the civil disobedience in the Kond Maliahs of Orissa. A comparatively recent rebellion in the Adilabad District of Hyderabad in 1941 was partly due to the alienation of Gond land."

Someone will quickly remark that tribal land is protected by legislation that no one is allowed to own land in tribal areas. K. Suresh Singh points out how in spite of Chotanagpur Tenancy Act, tribal land in that area continues to go into non-tribal hands. He says, "There has been a noticeable increase in the incidence of alienation of land in contravention of the Act in favour of other tribals and non-tribals, and both tribal and professional money-lenders have been active in the countryside. In fact many fraudulent devices of unlawfully acquiring possession of tribal lands have come to light."

Has something similar happened in North-East India? The misfortunes of the tribals have been the same all over the country. They continue to lose their land even to this day. There is general unhappiness. It finds expression in various forms from time to time. The extreme element takes to violence. In some places violence has been put down, but not everywhere, and not always to the same extent. Anyone sincerely wanting to know the rate of loss of tribal lands needs only to make a study of the non-tribal penetration of the tribal belt in Assam north of Brahmaputra. How much land have the Bodos lost? The Mikirs are probably even worse sufferers. The immigration rate into the Mikir and North Cachar Hills between 1951 and 1961 has been as high as 20.54%. The invasion continues.

Elwin describes the paradise that Arunachal was, "In NEFA there are no land lords, no extortionate money-lenders, no liquor vendors, merchants only in the foothills, and there is none of the economic impoverishment, the anxiety and the corruption that such people have brought to the other, more accessible, tribal areas." Every tribal area was in the same condition. But see how tribal belts and autonomous districts have benefited from the introduction of such invaluable contributions of non-tribal people. The classical example of the nation's concern for its tribal people is not NEFA, but Tripura. What a marvellous achievement of integration is a state where a people that owned the entire land have been reduced to less than a third of the population! They are daily retreating to the interior, with hardly any representation in the Government! How long will they continue to retreat before the invader? Time will tell.

Where tribal land has found sufficient protection, the people have suffered from other problems. Like in Bihar "they (the tribals) found their erstwhile exploiters, the non-tribal middle class got all the schemes and benefited most from the development projects. The block staff, most of whom belonged to non-tribal areas was corrupt and it was next to impossible for a tribal to get any grant, subsidy or loan from the block without greasing the palm of the penal officials" (Sachchidananda). The same writer says elsewhere, "Most of the funds meant for the tribals were cornered by the non-tribals," and again "Most of the big industries in tribal areas are owned either by the state or by non-tribal industrialists from outside Bihar." The situation has been exactly the same in Northeast India. And in spite of official denials, this situation tends to worsen.

The distorted understanding that some people have of "integration" has been another cause of problem. There are persons who identify "integration" with "assimilation" and even "absorption." according to some of the Hindu society. "Attempts to produce cultural uniformity and integration through induced assimilation can be dangerous" (M. N. Srinivas and R. D. Sanwal). If, then, trouble has arisen, it has been due to neglecting the warning of Pandit Nehru who said, "The problem of the tribal areas is to make the people feel that they have perfect freedom to live their own lives and to develop according to their wishes and genius. Any conception that India is ruling them and that they are ruled, or that customs and habits with which they are unfamiliar are going to be imposed upon them, will alienate them and make our frontier problem more difficult." That is precisely what happened. For, "a great deal of what is happening in NEHA today can be related to the tribal elite's fear of losing their cultural identity in an ocean of Hindu nationalism" (M. N. Srinivas and R. D. Sanwal).

As Roy Burman points out, the agitation against cow-slaughter, the adoption of Assamese as the state language, the "adoption of symbols of Hinduism in state functions, for instance, performance of puja at the time of inauguration of the Oil Refinery in Assam", etc. have not helped to remove the tribal peoples' fear. Ms. Terhuja refers to an incident at Khonoma village where one of the villagers was about to be killed by some Hindu military personnel for killing a cow.

The people know that the Government will try to Hinduise them to the extent it can. And that in spite of loud protestations of secularism, everyone knows what is happening in Arunachal Pradesh. S. Chaube admits that Christians of the hills and the Assam valley strongly resent the fact that Christianity alone is restricted in Arunachal, while Buddhism and Hinduism in particular are lavishly patronized. There is a strong feeling against people's blaming every trouble on Christianity. Nichols Roy says, "The attacks on the church by various individuals have brought about distrust."

■ ■ ■

What the Missionary Has Really Done

There is no need to say much here. Even those who criticize the Christians most, rush their children to missionary schools and their sick to Christian hospitals. The grief is that the same service should be done to the tribals. Those that are nobly minded have not been like that. D. R. Mankekar says, "India as a whole should be grateful to early Christian missionaries for helping these tribals to make a big leap forward from primitive life to modernity and thus taking off the over weighted shoulders of Independent

India that gigantic task and preparing them to take their due place in Indian polity." Gandhiji had a great esteem for the Christian educator. He says, "I believe in the ancient idea of teaching for the love of it and receiving the barest maintenance. The Roman Catholics have retained that idea and they are responsible for some of the best educational institutions in the world." The Christian missionary brought to the tribals education, health, sound and healthy habits, music, peace. He has given their languages a script, grammars and dictionaries and a literature.

S. C. Roy in his *The Mundas and Their Country* tells us what the missionaries have done for the Mundas through schools, colleges, trade schools, cooperatives, industrial schools, etc. Such institutions all over India serve Christians and non-Christians alike. Education also gave the tribal an appreciation of his democratic rights; it was the same thing that happened to the Indian elite. If this awareness led to painful consequences, the remedy should be sought elsewhere. Elwin's great fear was that missionary effort developed into an inferiority complex among the tribals. He said, "The fundamental objection to missionary effort, of whatever religion or even of social reform work, is that it greatly increases self-distrust." He found a Konyak and an interpreter from Tirap who were ashamed to be called Nagas. But today the accusation of visitors from outside is that the tribal Christians of Northeast India, Nagas included, are proud. They are proud to be what they are, they are proud to be Christians, they are proud of their separate identity. Are Christians bound to be always in the wrong?

When the Administration entered, the detribalization started under the impact of modern civilization; there was a spiritual vacuum which needed to be filled. Neither the administration nor the development officer nor the education inspector could have given what the missionary did. B. K. Roy Burman says, "In many areas Christianity appears to have served the role of filling up the intellectual and spiritual vacuum caused by the growing scepticism among the tribal population about their traditional faith and world view." And the missionary was not the iconoclast that he is often made out to be. Let an impartial authority judge whether Elwin's advice to officers was lived more by officers or by the missionaries. Nityananda Das says, "Elwin's 'Philosophy for NEFA' was distributed to all top officers all over the country. But can we say that any one has given serious thought to the prescriptions embodied in that book?"

Here are some of his prescriptions:

- "The best administrators of tribal people are, generally speaking, men of wide general education, men who read and think."
- He quotes Pandit Nehru: "The man who goes there (tribal area) as an officer must be prepared to enter their huts, talk to them, eat and smoke with them, live their lives and not consider himself superior or apart. Then only can he gain their confidence and respect, and then be in a position to advise them."
- "Humility has been the dominant virtue of the most successful administrators of tribal areas throughout the world."
- "In fact, patience and even temper are qualities admired even by the most warlike tribes."
- "They (tribal people) like to feel that an officer is a person of position, authority and dignity, but at the same time they expect him to mix freely with them on terms of equality: they expect him to be always accessible."

- "They appreciate any genuine interest in their customs and traditions and respond readily to the expression of admiration for their textiles and other arts."
- "Then again the tribal people are admirers of men and women who work hard."
- "Very important to tribal psychology is the love of truth and a belief in justice. The people expect him to tell the truth even if it is unpalatable and nothing causes greater trouble than for him to make promises which he cannot fulfil."
- "A knowledge of the language is the window by which we see into the tribal mind; it is the door through which we shall most readily receive affection and cooperation."
- And the last is from R. N. Haldipur: "They (administrators) have to become not only tribal-minded but also rural minded. Usually our officials are urban-oriented and do not like to work with their hands."

We would like to know who has been more faithful to the spirit behind this code, the administrator or the missionary. And if an administrator with these qualities can do real service in the tribal society, can no one else?

■ ■ ■

Do Figures Show an "Alarming Rate of Growth" of Christians?

Statistics are often quoted to prove that the Christian community in Northeast India is growing at an "alarming rate." But we must not be one-sided in the study of statistics. Let us look at the growth rate of other communities in Northeast India too. The table below shows the percentage of growth of religious communities from 1961 to 1971:

AREA	RELIGIOUS COMMUNITY	GROWTH %
1. Goalpara Dt.	Sikhs	182.26
2. Kamrup Dt.	Sikhs	127.23
3. Kamrup Dt.	Buddhists	282.04
4. North Cachar Dt.	Buddhists	843.75
5. Mizo Hills	Muslims	827.09
6. Mikir Hills	Hindus	86.08
7. Mikir Hills	Muslims	62.89
8. Manipur West	Hindus	820.00
9. Manipur North	Hindus	115.90
10. Manipur North	Sikhs	575.00
11. Manipur East	Muslims	130.77
12. Manipur East	Sikhs	433.33
13. Manipur East	Hindus	356.26
14. Garo Hills	Buddhists	215.52
15. Garo Hills	Jains	400.00
16. Kohima Dt.	Muslims	177.66
17. Kohima Dt.	Buddhists	233.08
18. Kohima Dt.	Sikhs	207.09
19. Mokokchung Dt.	Hindus	112.00
20. Tuensang	Hindus	119.49
21. Tuensang Dt.	Muslims	172.84
22. Tuensang Dt.	Jains	300.00
23. Tripura state	Sikhs	548.98

According to 1971 census there are in all the districts of Arunachal Pradesh a considerable percentage of Hindus; in Kameng (19.68%), in Subansiri (13.32%), in Lohit (49.96%). In Elwin's survey of NEFA tribes in the late fifties we find no reference to the Hindus in the territory except among the Noctes of Tirap. Who evangelized these others? Or are they settlers from outside tribal territory? Or, is it that the census has been manipulated? Probably, all three happened. And this is in spite of the fact that Elwin's philosophy was the slogan of the administration all these years.

"The NEFA Administration observes a policy of strict religious neutrality and would not impose even tribal religion on those who do not want it. It takes exactly the same attitude to the Hindu, Buddhist or Muslim missionaries as it does to Christian missionaries. In frontier areas, it has been felt wise not to disturb the people with new forms of religion which may puzzle them and which may even compete with one another for allegiance" (*A Philosophy for NEFA*, Verrier Elwin). The author considered it completely wrong that "officials, servants of a secular state, should use their position to promote their own religion, whatever that might be." But it happened.

There is a misconception among the majority in the country that the population growth of Christians in India is alarming. To the contrary, census data shows a fall from 2.44% to 2.30% in growth figures between 2001 and 2011. Moreover, Christians constitute only 2% of India's population.

Christianity introduced and established some of the best schools and colleges with very high standards of education in India. Charitable hospitals and health centres and homes for the destitute, the elderly, orphans and lepers serve people throughout the length and breadth of the country. While availing facilities in such Christian institutions, people are not discriminated against on the basis of religious belief and faith.

■ ■ ■

Is Isolation the Solution?

There are die hard anthropologists who will argue that absolutely nothing in the tribal society should be touched. J. P. Mills in 1931 lamented the suppression of head hunting. He said, "The suppression of head hunting though necessary in an area which is fully administered, has probably been not for the benefit of the tribes. The number of lives saved by the suppression of the practice is therefore negligible, and it is more than balanced by those lost through the spread of disease made easy by safe travelling everywhere. In addition to this there is a real loss in virility and keenness." It is true that the abolition of this dreadful practice led to the decay of certain types of dances, personal ornamentation and tattooing, wood carving and funerary ceremonials. In spite of all this loss, there are those who will shed a tear over the disappearance of head hunting. Most thinking men today admit that isolation is no solution.

Dr. B. S. Guha wrote in 1951, "Complete isolation has never led to the progress and advancement, but always to stagnation and death whether we look to lower animals or human beings."

Elwin convincingly argues that isolation is impossible in the modern world, and would be desirable even if it was possible, "The old controversy about zoos and museums has long been dead. We do not want to preserve tribal culture in its colour and beauty to interest the scientist, or attract the tourists." Even the partial isolation policy has been so often attacked by all sections of people that we need not dwell long on the demerits of total isolation.

■ ■ ■

***A Philosophy for NEFA* by Elwin—A Liability or an Asset?**
One would have thought that the condition of the tribals in Arunachal Pradesh would be the happiest where the "Philosopher" was "King." But not all philosophy can be translated into action. That is what happened with *A Philosophy for*

NEFA. The philosophy has been contradictory; in practice, it had to stumble. The author is the arch-enemy of detribalization. But then he praises the Administration which "takes school boys on tours round India and sends parties regularly to New Delhi on great occasions; it is awarding stipends to its outstanding boys and girls to study in various parts of India." The consequence is what he himself indicates on the next page, "The man who has gone out to the mines, or the youth takes from his community and put into a school, considers himself free of, and indeed, superior to the laws, regulations and customs of his 'backward' parents and relations."

R. N. Haldipur says something similar about educated tribal youth in general, "But they return like strangers who unconsciously react to the shoddy appearance of their home and the villages and are like square pegs in round holes." And as Elwin says "They will not easily put up with a system of taboos which prevents them from going about, or weaving when they want to, or working in the fields at just the right time. They may come to feel that the older people are obstacles to progress."

It is evident that the educated will be impatient of slavery, inequality, the bride-price system, and taboos. "They may, if the elders are not obstructive, destroy much that is good along with the bad" (Elwin). He admits elsewhere, "Education, however, under any circumstance, is bound to be disturbing, and of the one problem it creates is a conflict between generations." So detribalization had fast begun under the Administration's monopoly rule in Arunachal Pradesh.

Nor is it only education that can be disturbing in tribal areas. Nityananda Das speaking of Orissa says, "The electoral system based on the adult franchise introduced in almost all the tribal areas produced new leaders on totally a different perspective."

And again he says, "Opening of industries and introduction of innovations and communications has changed social values,"

The same thing happened among the tribals of Bihar. "They go to the tea gardens of Assam and North Bengal; to the jute mills and brick kilns about Calcutta, they have been thrown into the vortex of industrialism and have been exposed to new influences, values, attitudes and beliefs" (Sachchidananda).

So whatever benefits the administration may be bringing to the tribal people, whether it is education, industry, adult franchise, or money economy, it can be disturbing, and it can have a detribalizing effect.

Elwin's philosophy, no doubt very well intentioned, is full of contradictions. The trouble is that he is an anthropologist, a philosopher and an adviser to the administration at the same time. At one moment he is an idealist, and at another a realist. For example, in one place he stands firmly against detribalization. He has a full chapter on the social, political, aesthetic, economic, hygienic aspects and on the problem of dress. But at another place he says, "We must recognize the fact that a certain number of tribal boys and girls will become largely 'modernized', at all events, in such externals as dress and general style of living. These will be the political officers, the politicians, the doctors and lawyers, the engineers of the future," But then he will not concede that man tends to imitate the elite in his society and tries to take after them at the earliest opportunity he can. Then finally he concludes, "The problem of dress is only part of a much bigger problem of detribalization as a whole." It is no good trying to preserve and develop tribal dress unless there is overall growth, he realizes he is fighting a hopeless case, and gives up, "Detribalization of a kind and some degree, as I have already pointed out, will be inevitable in certain cases. The boy who goes to the university, who will be trained up to be a future superintending engineer, director of health services, or advisor to the governor, will wear whatever dress convention dictates at the time and live in the same style as officers from other parts of India. And this will do no harm, provided such detribalization has come about naturally and not as a reaction against a despised past or a system of inferiority complex." Is it that the detribalization that takes place at the hands of the administration alone that will do no harm?

At another place Elwin quotes an anonymous memorandum on "The Impact of Modern Civilization on the Tribal Peoples of Madhya Pradesh" in order to strengthen his arguments. It reads, "Not only has contact with a higher civilization this (harmful) effect in the moral realm but it is equally disastrous in that of craftsmanship." But he knows that the "middle way" he is advocating is hardly workable and becomes a realist and an administrator when he says, "Yet there are more important things than 'culture' and I believe the greatest gift—and that too the gift must appreciated—which the Administration has brought to NEFA is the gift of peace." You have brought peace indeed! But then, you set in motion a process of detribalization. It was the same thing that happened in other parts of Northeast India too, and with the same results. And the missionary had nothing to do with it.

Are we accusing the administration? Far from it. We only want to know who began the detribalization process. Elwin speaks of areas where the administration wanted to introduce reforms: "In NEFA at least the people had not enough food; they suffered from abominable diseases; they died young; they were heavily burdened with anxiety; their life was destructed by war, kidnapping, slavery and cruel punishments." Here the administrator in Elwin prevails. No agency can enter into any of these fields without tampering with elements that are vital to a culture. But then there are "more important things than culture." We agree. Only, why blame others for what you have done?

■ ■ ■

Freedom to Choose

Elwin claimed to be a missionary of Pandit Nehru's views on tribal affairs. In all honesty we must admit that Panditji was far more clear and consistent than his missionary. He did not try merely to philosophize, but his love and concern for the tribals were evident in all his contacts and statements. He said, "The Government of India is determined to help the tribal people grow according to their own genius and tradition; it is not the intention to impose anything on them." A freedom-fighter like Nehru knew how to respect the freedom of the tribal people.

Dr. Rajendra Prasad had similar sentiments on the same issue. He said, "My own idea is that facilities for education and for general improvement in their economic life should be provided for them and it should be left to them to choose whether they would like to be assimilated with, and absorbed by the surrounding society, or would like to maintain their own separate tribal existence." If they choose to merge with the rest of the people, they will be detribalized, it is true, but at least it is their own choice and they are free to shape their own destiny as they please.

"Free" intermingling or cultures has always been beneficial. Dr. B. S. Guha says, "So long as the borrowing has been natural and in harmony with cultural setting and the psychological make-up of the people, it has been eminently beneficial and even added to their richness of their culture." But unfortunately such a wise policy, so nobly conceived by the leaders of the nation, was never carried out.

In the case of Arunachal Pradesh, while all types of barriers were placed in the way of the Christians, Hinduism was not only officially favoured, but an attempt was even made to force it down on the tribal people. Nehru said, "I am alarmed when I see—not only in this country, but in other great countries too—how anxious people are to shape others according to their own image or likeness, and to impose on them their particular way of living." Yes! We are alarmed today!

■ ■ ■

The Unsecular Face of Secular India

Hinduism is a great religion, its tenets most admirable, its philosophy most noble and its devotional practices most inspiring. But for all its beauty, no one would like it to be rammed down his throat against his wishes. That is what the Government of India and the Government of Arunachal Pradesh tried to do during the last few decades.

Somehow the centre has the impression that by Hinduising the people of Arunachal Pradesh, you make them better Indians. Ashrams, temples and a number of mission schools have been opened at huge government expense.

The 1953 cabinet decision of the Government of India prohibiting Christian missionaries in NEFA, now Arunachal Pradesh, strengthened the hands of the local administration for adopting an anti-Christian stance. Of late, the Hinduisation efforts of the Government have increased with the mushrooming growth of Hindu schools taking advantage of the isolation of the Union Territory (kept isolated, of course, on purpose) to apply cultural and educational pressures on the people to accept Hinduism.

The Government is doing the very thing that they claim they want to prevent. They are taking advantage of the people and leaders. During the heyday of persecutions of Christians, many of the leaders in Arunachal Pradesh knew so little how democracy functions and what type of India we all belong to.

■ ■ ■

Is Hinduisation a Solution?

"Some seem to suggest that the process of assimilation with Hinduism which has been going on in India over the ages should be encouraged" (M. N. Srinivas and R. D. Sanwal). Is It true that the tribal problem would have been non-existent, that the tribals would have been in the happiest situation if the Hinduisation process had continued? There is no doubt that Hinduism has a great power of absorption and many tribes of Northeast India were gradually coming to the Hindu fold until recent years, though we have no evidence to suggest that any of the Naga, Mizo or the Arunachal tribes were to any degree influenced by that great religion.

And how do a people get admission into a Hindu society? D. N. Majumdar says, "I believe that the Hindu caste structure is a device by which groups at the periphery of Hinduism (tribes) are accepted into the greater Hindu society." Speaking of the Bodo tribes he pointed out how the Dalus have already become a full-fledged Hindu caste. The Hinduisation process is also called the Sanskritization process. So the Rabhas, the Koches and the Hajongs, who are undergoing the process, are occupying an intermediary stage between the tribe and the caste. Thus they are being detribalized.

D. N. Majumdar describes the stage in full detail, "The process of Sanskritization starts with the simple claim of a group as being members of the greater Hindu society. This varies in direct proportion with the abandonment of the 'unclean' 'non-Hindu' habits, the foremost of which is beef-eating." So first beef-eating is given up, then the keeping of and later even the eating of pork and fowl ceases. Neighbouring Hindus accept the group more and more as they give up all these "unclean" habits.

At the next stage the tribe abandons non-Hindu deities and adopts the deities of the Hindu pantheon and traditional rites. The rites to deities such as Kali, Durga and Saraswati call for a Brahmin priest. But non-Brahmin priestly services are sometimes tolerated. As time passes people begin to give up all the major elements of tribal social customs (at birth, marriage and death) and adopt traditional Hindu rites performed by a professional Brahmin. Now they have reached a high degree of Sanskritization. Finally the adoption of an Aryan language crowns the process. They have been, meanwhile, completely detribalized. They have lost everything they had. Elwin says, "Hindu reformers, who teach vegetarianism and teetotalism as well as a number of taboos and customs hitherto unknown to tribal society, are equally destructive to village unity."

And what is worse, they will have paid a very high price for their admission into the Hindu fold: they will be assigned to the lowest position there. Elwin says, "throughout tribal India there is a tendency towards the transformation of tribes into castes, and these 'castes' are usually at the bottom of the social scale." The anonymous memorandum of the tribals of Madhya Pradesh quoted earlier says, "In the immediate neighbourhood of Kondagaon there are villages occupied by tribal people who are now virtually in process of detribalization. One of the results of this process is that, while it is a declared policy of the Government to abolish casteism, casteism is here in the making. Such tribal people have worked out a caste relationship the one with the other, and for all with the structure of the surrounding Hindu population the result of which is that each one forms a caste below the other and all below the lowest neighbouring Hindu caste."

So "in the Brahmaputra valley Koch, formerly the name of the tribe, has become a caste which admits proselytes to Hinduism from the ranks of the Kacharis and other aboriginal tribes" (Gait). The Jaintia Rajas and nobles under the influence of Brahmins had joined the Sakta sect, and had zealously begun performing human sacrifices according to the prescriptions of *Kalika Purana*.

Thus it hardly seems that Hinduisation would have been the solution to the tribal problem. At best they would have joined the mute and oppressed millions of Indians with the sole privilege of being called *"Harijans."*

■ ■ ■

The Tragedy of Arunachal Pradesh (NEFA)

The NEFA philosophy was to be a guide to all young officers in tribal areas throughout India; today the NEFA scandal is a standing disgrace to a nation that professes democracy and secularism. To begin with we must admit that the spirit that has inspired the author of *A Philosophy for NEFA* and Pandit Nehru, who gave it the official approval, was truly admirable. But that philosophy was doomed to failure because nobody could see the "Middle Way" that Elwin was advocating, especially when it came to making concrete on the spot decisions, and partly because the whole thing was given a pro-Hindu, anti-Christian bias from the beginning.

First of all, too much of a myth is being built up about the marvels that the administration has accomplished in Arunachal Pradesh. Nobody knows for certain all that is happening behind the "Iron Curtain," for a veritable Iron Curtain hangs at the state borders. Official reports contain miracles, performed on paper probably rather than in reality. But other versions become available from time to time when some rare visitor to the Union Territory succeeds to verify facts on personal observation, and has the courage to report what he has seen. Major Sita Ram Johri, for instance says, "The more a visitor penetrates into the Indo-Burmese border areas (in Tirap), the more horrid pictures of poverty, ignorance and filth he sees." He is shocked at the inefficiency of the Administration. A number of officers are mere drones. Pandit Nehru said, "What I am anxious about particularly is to avoid large number of outsiders being sent to the tribal areas in some capacity or other." District Research Officers who are totally incapable of producing any worthwhile work have been drawing fat salaries. "It is high time that these DRO's are removed from the NEFA Administration" (Major Sita Ram Johri).

About the much praised single-line administration Major Johri says that it was obsolete even in 1959. Quoting the National Council of Applied Economics Research, S. Chaube says the same thing, "The present single-line system has become outdated. Under this system, the district administrative is vested with enormous powers which he cannot efficiently use. It also leads to wasteful practices and delays." Dr. D. Ering, himself an Arunachalee, had much stronger words about the single-line administration. He says, "This sort of an administrative set-up in NEFA was started in 1955 and is continuing till date. This has not yielded any good result but has brought degeneration in the rank and file of the technical departments. It has bred disloyalties at every level of the Government employees. The single-line administrative set up in NEFA has made the Deputy Commissioners and his junior administrative officers all-knowing, all-seeing and all pervading." The Chief Commissioner of the Union Territory (now the Lt. Governor) and these subordinate officers enjoy powers that hardly the most ambitious colonial officers exercised in the heyday of colonialism.

No matter how great the miracles that the administration is working, freedom is precious to the people. That cannot be suppressed forever without inviting trouble. People do not like to have anything imposed on them, not even services. Roy Burman says, "But it should be realized that in the context of modern democracy, there is an optimum level beyond which good administration and amenities cannot be provided, without broad-based participation of the population concerned in the decision making process at different levels." The high handed ways of the officers are actually alienating the population. For example, the Devanagiri Script, which was suitable for central Indian languages, was imposed on all the NEFA dialects. But "The eastern hill men prefer the Roman Script. NEFA has not got any opportunity to express its choice" (S. Chaube). The indigenous populations "are incapable of raising their voice. If they make a complaint it remains within the borders of the district" (Major Sita Ram Johri). The other unwise policy of settling refugees and retired defence personnel in the Union Territory is bound to create trouble. How long will the Iron Curtain remain?

The administration has been frantically worried about the leakage of information through the borders. The Inner Line today keeps any thinking man from crossing the state borders. Harish Chandola, a journalist, wrote, "Why is the Inner Line here today: I am afraid it is there to prevent thinking people from going in. Otherwise, I have known most objectionable characters taken in by some officers who consider themselves owners of the frontier."

But absolute power tries to hold on as long as it can. The term of office of the Chief Commissioner was repeatedly extended. (Here we pass over in silence the farce of an election last year in the Union Territory; how the opposition was not allowed to canvass in most places, how they were not allowed to place their men at the booths, how the simple voter was clearly told where to put the rubber stamp.) We pass over the scandal of the en mass walk-over of the Congress Party in Arunachal Pradesh to the Janata camp, so cleverly done under the direction of K. A. A. Raja, the Lt. Governor so that he could continue his anti-Christian policies. We do not wish to make even a casual reference to the school boy type of behaviour of the Ministers before the Lt. Governor or to what extent they are his mere puppets and spokesmen, nor even to the fact that the entire anti-Christian programme in Arunachal Pradesh has been masterminded in the Home Ministry, New Delhi.

The administration, throwing the principles of Elwin to the winds, has been hurriedly preparing a set of officers who will continue the one-sided policy it has adopted, "education is alienating the youth from their social milieu and is turning them into sycophants of the administration." But not all young men can be bluffed into anything. There are people who see through the fallacies of NEFA philosophy and its questionable execution. Birendra Kumar Bhattacharya says, "His 'A Philosophy for NEFA' (now Arunachal) is more likely to be treated as a philosophy of stagnation rather than of progress. Very few Arunachal young men follow his prescriptions on preservation of cultures, reform of tribal religions, dress and hut-house cultural growth." The trouble is yet to begin in Arunachal Pradesh and the Administration has sown the seeds of several varieties of them.

■ ■ ■

The Underground Church

Christianity was introduced into Arunachal Pradesh long before Independence. The Bible had not been printed in tribal dialects, but hand written copies were already in circulation. "After the advent of the Indian administration the manuscripts were hidden but at heart many Adi families remained Christians" (Major Sita Ram Johri). This comes as a shock to many a Christian in other parts of India. Where was the need of hiding the Bible in this democratic secular state? Does not the constitution of India guarantee "liberty of thought, expression, belief, faith and worship"? But the Adi Christians had to go underground for survival. They were too few and too weak. "In 1959 I noticed that educated Adi young men and many families did not admit that they were Christians" (Johri). Christians increase under persecutions. "Now it is an accepted fact that Christians dominate the Pasighat area" (Johri).

Christian students were refused stipends. Further, "administration stopped sanctioning stipends to boys who wanted to go to Missionary Colleges for higher education" (S. Chaube). An Arunachal Christian can read these words of the Indian Constitution only with tears in his eyes: Article 15 (1) "The state shall not discriminate against any citizen on grounds only of religion, race, caste, sex, place of birth or any of them." Since 1961 several Arunachal tribes had adherents to Christianity. They were Nyishis, Gallongs, Mijus, Mikirs, Miniyongs, Miris, Mishings, Padams, Pasis, Tagians, Noctes, Tangsa, Mishmis and Monpas, and yet no Christian priest or pastor was allowed to visit them or give them the consolations of religion. The fear was that the priest would propagate his faith. But Christians were already long present in the Union Territory. Does Article 25 (1) of the Indian Constitution where it says, "All persons are equally entitled to freedom of conscience and the right freely to profess, practice and propagate religion" extend to Arunachal Pradesh?

We would like to emphasize the word "equally." For what was refused to Christianity was allotted to Hinduism in tenfold measure. The administration thought that it would be safest to entrust the education of the Union Territory to Rama Krishna Mission, and large numbers of students were sent to Rama Krishna Mission institutions throughout the country so that they might pray and offer puja at the State's expense. Young men have been entrusted to Hindu families. Such youths belonged to the privileged group, and get not only their stipends, scholarships and allowances, but also travel by air, and are the pride of the administration. While Christian communities that already existed in the Union Territory were not allowed to open any institution or have a place of worship, the Rama Krishna Mission was asked to open a school in Along and another in Tirap. Others are in the making. The tribes were not enthusiastic. Major Sita Ram Johri frankly admits, "They suspect that the Government might be trying to Hinduise their children." Elwin had said long ago that Hinduism was not to the liking of Arunachal people. He said, "I doubt if the NEFA people will accept Hinduism in any organized manner. Between them and that great religion stands the gentle figure of the cow, the tribal people even educated ones will not give up their mithun, beef and beer; they are likely to reject the caste system, the new and unfamiliar taboos, the prevailing Puritanism." And yet this unconstitutional effort at Hinduisation continues.

Major Sita Ram Johri speaks of a Hindu organization called Shanti Sena operating in Tirap, Siang and Subansiri. It has also a women's branch that runs ashrams. Why is the Christian community not allowed to have their own spiritual and educational centres in the Union Territory? According to 1961 census 23.6% of the Padams and 5.70% of the Miniyongs were Christians. Today there are many more. Are they not citizens of India? Are their rights not guaranteed by the constitution? Article 30 (1) of the constitution reads, "All minorities, whether based on religion or language, shall have the right to establish and administer educational institutions of their choice." Major Sita Ram Johri reports the case of a student who studied in a Mission School in Darjeeling and fell into the bad books of the Administration. The administration is reported as trying every stratagem to send him to a Rama Krishna Mission School in Bengal despite the boy's stiff resistance. The condition now is that anyone who studied in Christian institutions finds it impossible to continue his studies under the patronage of the administration, even if his standard is much higher, except, of course, the corrective course under the supervision of the Rama Krishna Mission. Nay more, he will get no job, and is likely to be harassed for the rest of his life. In general the administration frowns on all who studied in Shillong for fear of "Christian" influence. It is good to be reminded that Shillong is the centre of the North Eastern Hill University and also that many Arunachali officers are still in that town. Yet it is considered a "dangerous" place to study in.

Major Sita Ram Johri says, when he was in Tirap, "on enquiry I found that a Vaishnav priest from the plains visited his Nocte disciples once a year. He held religious discourses for a week, collected tributes from his followers and returned to his centre." In one place Major Johri noticed that there were only a few attendants at religious services. The *"prasad"* was not attractive enough. "I suggested that *peras*, an Indian sweetmeat, should replace gram. This innovation might attract devotees to the Namghar in a large number. It would cost the administration Rs. 50 per month. The D. C. accepted the suggestion." Alas for the secular state we live in! Does the tax payer know that his money goes for the maintenance of Hindu religious worship in Arunachal Pradesh? Would that Gandhiji were alive today, who said, "We have suffered enough from a state-aided religion and a church."

An interesting aspect is the effort of the administration to Hinduise not only the people but also the tribal Gods. "There is now a conscious effort among some officials to bring the indigenous religious faiths into a close proximity to Hinduism. An interesting example is furnished by a Bharat darshan (tour of India) in early 1968 which brought some Adis in contact with a Hindu sage of southern India who gave them images of their supreme Gods Donyi Polo (the sun and the moon). The temple of the gods who in the Adis pristine religion, had no images for worship, was built with much fanfare in a more or less Hindu way" (S. Chaube). Thus a Hindu temple was built in Hindu style to the Adi god. The Adis wanted to offer a mithun in sacrifice; they were not allowed. They resented the sacred symbol *OM* at the entrance, and after prolonged protests it was removed. What a farce these officers (by the way, the best qualification for getting a job in the Arunachal Administration is anti-Christian fanaticism) have made of Elwin's philosophy, the secular image of India and the nation's respect for minorities.

It is no secret that Christianity has made an appeal to the hill people of North East India. "Christianity has made an appeal to the hill people of Assam because it has been associated in their minds with the idea of progress" (Elwin). S. Chaube confirms this view. It is then no wonder that the little Christian community that existed in Arunachal Pradesh steadily grew over the years. Though the Christians grew in numbers, Christian religious worship was completely forbidden. Repeatedly the Administration got anti-social elements to burn them down. The big jobs, remunerative contracts, and the favour of the Government await those who are willing to follow its anti-Christian policy. Major Johri says that it is an accepted fact that Pasighat area is dominated by Christians. Could, then, the church of the bamboo and wood which they built in 1974 at great expense and trouble be burnt down without the Administration's active encouragement? And who were imprisoned? The builders, not the criminals. Three of the builders were detained for a week as a strong warning. Under the single-line administration, the blame for such cases of misgovernment extended because of his "wise" policies. What is particularly interesting to note is that in Pasighat there are shrines of every religious group but not of the Christians, though they "dominate the Pasighat area."

The spy system in Arunachal Pradesh is second only to that in communist countries. Christians are followed everywhere. Students from Christian schools are shadowed. Personal mail is opened. And everything is recorded. Why this persecution of the Christian minority? Is Hinduism the best guarantee of loyalty to India? Then Nepal would have been India. Is religion the one uniting force in a country? Then Bangladesh would have still been a part of Pakistan. Tolerance was eminently an Indian virtue which today is forgotten. Long ago Gandhiji had said, "I do not expect India on my dreams to develop one religion, i.e. to be wholly Hindu, or wholly Christian, or wholly Musalman, but I want it to be wholly tolerant, with its religions working side by side with one another."

How far we have come from Gandhi's ideals!

But the worst happened in 1974, when the Arunachal Council, which everyone knows was the personal creation of the Chief Commissioner and applauded anything he decreed, urged the administration to take up steps to see that all Christians abjured their faith by January 26, 1975. The Council, on behalf of the Chief Commissioner issued warning of dire consequences to the recalcitrant: "expulsion from their society, denial of all benefits and privileges of holding land, settlement within the Territory of Arunachal Pradesh, and award of stipends and scholarships." The Council

Resolution said, "on the occasion of the performance of certain rites and ceremonies locally in villages, every local (the converted or traditional) must participate whole heartedly, failing which, he or she would be dealt with accordingly to establish tenets of our customary law." Who interprets the customary law? The outsider.

The tribal people are not much upset about a mature person changing his religion. "Alien" officers (self appointed guardians of tribal culture) will decide what penalties should be inflicted for the violation of imagined tribal laws. So the Christians have been refused employment, licenses and permits for trade and business, stipends and scholarships; he will be ostracized, deprived of his paternal inheritance, and the right of residence in his own state. Let some legal expert in tribal law tell us whether such are the punishments that "customary law" assigns to those who change their religion.

The Christian community feels very insecure. They have already suffered much for their faith. Their churches have been burnt down, they have been spied upon, and they have been refused stipends and scholarships. They have been imprisoned, tortured and at least one has been killed. We cannot mention their names for the same reason that escapees from communist countries have refused to give particulars. But we have unimpeachable evidence of active persecution of Christians in all the forms mentioned above.

This cannot go on. We feel that three decades of suffering is long enough under a democratic secular Government. We want to know whether the Constitution of India extends to Arunachal Pradesh. If it does, we want our rights defended. While the Government is insisting that certain dissident groups in North East India should work out solutions to their problems within the framework of the constitution of India, it is positively excluding Arunachal Pradesh from the same. What lessons should we draw from that?

6

AN UNWISE BILL—FREEDOM OF RELIGION BILL
By Rajmohan Gandhi (*Himmat* March 30, 1979)

At the first glance Mr. O. P. Tyagi's Bill providing for "prohibition of conversion from one religion to another by the use of force or inducement or by fraudulent means" appears innocuous. But reflection shows that it is capable, if enacted, of seriously curbing the right our Constitution gives to an individual to profess, practice and propagate the religion of his choice. The fears regarding the Bill expressed by a number of individuals and groups of men then become understandable.

Mr. Tyagi's Bill lays down that no person "shall convert or attempt to convert, either directly or otherwise, any person from one religious faith to another by the use of force or by inducement or by deceit or by any fraudulent means nor shall any person abet any such conversion."

Any conversion attained by force, bribery or trickery doubtless deserves reproof. How should improprieties of this kind dealt with? Intimidation and fraud are crimes that can be punished under the ordinary law. A special law in a field affecting religion has far reaching implications.

Such a law will enable politicians, pressure groups and District officials, if they are so minded; to harass those engaged peacefully and honourably in the propagation of their faith. The latter would be in constant fear of their daily duties being interpreted as some sort of "punishable inducement" or "force."

In Mr. Tyagi's Bill inducement "shall include the offer of any gift or gratification either in cash or in kind and shall also include the grant of any benefit, either pecuniary or otherwise." If someone among Calcutta's starving and dying cared for by Mother Teresa and her sisters were to ask to be baptized as a Christian, would Mother Teresa and her nuns go to jail for having "induced" the conversion by feeding and nursing him? Would teachers in colleges and doctors in hospitals be similarly liable if one of those "benefiting" by their training or service wished to change his religion?

A change in religion or indeed several such changes during one's life time are a right guaranteed by the Constitution. A thousand men may deplore the conversion of X from Christianity to Hinduism or vice-versa but X has a right in a democracy such as ours to go through it, or if he wishes to change his faith again in the future or become an atheist or a propagator of atheism. Giving to thousands of Government officials (and therefore to their political rulers) the power to decide that a particular conversion is not genuine, which is what the Bill would in effect do, is a hazardous proposition.

Individuals including leaders seem frequently to change their parties, perhaps in some cases under pecuniary inducement or a threat. There is no special law to prohibit such changes in political loyalties howsoever deplorable they may appear to be. All Indian citizens have the right to their political beliefs without state interference. Their equally important right to believe in and belong to any religion of their choice should not be threatened directly or indirectly.

In his statement of the Bill's objects and reasons, Mr. Tyagi refers to the importance of providing against improper conversions to members of the scheduled cast and tribes. There is an assumption here that members of such groups are less capable than the others of deciding their religion for themselves. Irrespective of the validity of such a view it should be noted that they can freely move today from one political party to another. Would Mr. Tyagi like "safeguards" against such switches?

As far as Maharashtra is concerned, his bill would lead to demands for action under it against Hindus who seek to welcome back into their fold the Harijans who have turned Buddhist, and against Buddhist who strive to enlist more Hindu Harijans in their ranks.

"Nor shall any person abet any such conversion" is a phrase that would have the effect of turning a change of faith into a dangerous step inviting punishment at the hands of the State and social isolation.

Mr. Tyagi's Bill is similar in many respects to the Arunachal Pradesh Freedom of Indigenous Faith Act of 1978 which created a major controversy in much of the North-East. Unfortunately Arunachal and some other North-East States have witnessed mistrust and friction between Christian and Non-Christian communities from time to time. Some men in the region practicing their Indigenous faiths have been unhappy with the growth of the Christian community, and the latter has alleged discrimination and persecution.

I believe that the passage of Mr. Tyagi's Bill would be a remedy worse than the disease. State intervention in matters effecting in individual's innermost beliefs is not the answer to the problem of insincere conversions. The Janata Party, elected on the slogan of Human Liberty, ought not to endorse Mr. Tyagi's private Bill. Weight also should be given to the consideration that whatever its motives, the Bill is creating ill-feeling between communities.

* Rajmohan Gandhi is the grandson of the Father of the Nation, Mahatma Gandhi.

7

ARUNACHAL PRADESH FREEDOM OF RELIGION ACT, 1978, AND RELATED DOCUMENTS

The Arunachal Pradesh Freedom Of Religion Act, 1978

(Act No. 4 of 1978)

(Received the assent of the President of India on 25th Oct, 1978)

AN

ACT

to provide for prohibition of conversion from one religious faith to any other religious faith by use of force or inducement or by fraudulent means and for matters connected therewith.

Be it enacted by the Legislative Assembly of Arunachal Pradesh in the Twenty-ninth Year of the Republic of India as follows:-

1. (1) This act may be called the Arunachal Pradesh Freedom of Religion Act, 1978.
   (2) It extends to the whole of the Union Territory of Arunachal Pradesh.
   (3) It shall come into force at once.
2. In this Act, unless the context otherwise requires-
   (a) "Government" means the Government of the Union Territory of Arunachal Pradesh;
   (b) "Conversion" means renouncing one religious faith and adopting another religious faith, and "convert" shall be constructed accordingly;
   (c) "Indigenous faith" means such religions, beliefs and practices including rites, rituals, festivals. Observances, performances, abstinence, customs as have been found sanctioned, approved, performed by the indigenous communities of Arunachal Pradesh from the time these communities have been known and includes Buddhism as prevalent among the Monpas, Membas, Sherdukpens, Khambas, Khamptis and Singphos, Vaishnavism as practiced by Noctes, Akas and Nature worships, including worships of Donyi-Polo, as prevalent among other indigenous communities of Arunachal Pradesh;
   (d) "force" shall include show of force or a threat of injury any kind including threat of divine displeasure or social ex-communication;
   (e) "fraud" shall include the misrepresentation or any other fraudulent contrivance;
   (f) "inducement" shall include the offer of any gift or gratification, either in cash or in kind and shall also include the grant of any benefit, either pecuniary or otherwise;
   (g) "prescribed" means prescribed under the rules;
   (h) "religious faith" includes any indigenous faith.

3. No person shall convert or attempt to convert, either directly or otherwise, any person from one religious faith by the use of force or by inducement or by any fraudulent means nor shall any persons abet any such conversion.
4. Any person contravening the provisions contained in section 3, shall without prejudice to any civil liability, be punishable with imprisonment to the extent of two years and fine up to ten thousand rupees.
5. (1) Whoever converts any person from one religious faith to any other religious faith either by performing himself the ceremony necessary for such conversion as a religious priest or by taking part directly or indirectly in such ceremony shall, within such period after the ceremony as may be prescribed, send an intimation to the Deputy Commissioner of the District to which the person converted belongs, of the fact of such conversion in such form as may be prescribed.
   (2) If any person fails without sufficient cause to comply with the provisions contained in sub-section (1) he shall be punished with imprisonment which may extend to one year or with fine which may extend to one thousand rupees or with both.
6. An office under this Act shall be cognizable and shall not be investigated by an officer below the rank of an Inspector of Police.
7. No prosecution for an offence under this Act shall be instituted except by or with the previous sanction of the Deputy Commissioner or such other authority, not below the rank of an Extra Assistant Commissioner as may be authorized by him in this behalf.
8. The Government may make rules for the purpose of carrying out the provisions of this Act.

Note: Published in the Arunachal Pradesh Gazette, Extraordinary Part III, Vol. II, No. 22 Dated 13th November 1978

■ ■ ■

THE ARUNACHAL PRADESH GAZETTE
EXTRAORDINARY
PUBLISHED BY AUTHORITY
PART LLI

Vol.11, No.49, Itanagar, Wednesday, September 12, 1979.
Bhadra 21, 1901 (Saka)

GOVERNMENT OF ARUNACHAL PRADESH
POLITICAL DEPARTMENT
NOTIFICATION

The 12th Sep '79.

No. Pol.126/78—The following rules made under the Arunachal Pradesh Freedom of Religion Act, 1978 (No.4 of 1978) by the Government of Union Territory of Arunachal Pradesh are hereby published for general information.

(AS APPROVED BY THE GOVERNMENT ON 4TH SEPTEMBER, 1979)

THE ARUNACHAL PRADESH
FREEDOM OF RELIGION
RULES, 1979

In exercise of power conferred by Section 8 of the Arunachal Pradesh Freedom of Religion Act, 1978 (No.4 of 1978), the

Government of Union Territory of Arunachal Pradesh hereby makes the following rules, namely:-

RULES

1. Short title - These rules may be called the Arunachal Pradesh Religion Rules, 1979
2. Definitions - In these Rules, unless the context or otherwise requires -
   (a) "Act" means the Arunachal Pradesh Freedom of Religion Act, 1978 (No.4 of 1978)
   (b) "Form" means a Form appended to these rules;
   (c) "Government" means the Government of Arunachal Pradesh;
   (d) "Intimation" means the intimation in respect to conversion required to be given under sub-section (1) of Section 5 of the Act
3. Period within which intimation to be sent -
   (1) The intimation shall be sent to the DC of the District (to which the person converted belongs) within seven days after the date of such ceremony.
   (2) The intimation shall be Form A and shall be delivered either personally by the person giving such intimation to the DC or be sent to him by registered post with acknowledgement due.
4. Deputy Commissioner to issue acknowledgement receipt— The DC on receiving the intimation shall sign thereon a certificate stating the date on which and the hour at which the intimation has been delivered to him or received by him and shall for with acknowledge the receipt thereon in Form B.

5. Register of Conversion—The DC shall maintain a register of conversion from one religious faith to another in Form C and shall enter therein particulars of the intimations received by him.
6. Submission of report to Government—The DC shall, by the 10th of each month, send to the Government a report of intimations received by him during the preceding month in Form D.

■ ■ ■

The Arunachal Pradesh Extraordinary Gazette,
September 12, 1979

FORM A
(See Rule 3 (2))
Intimation regarding conversion from one religious faith to another

To
    The Deputy Commissioner
    District _____
    Arunachal Pradesh.

Sir,
I having performed the necessary ceremony for conversion as a religious priest/having taken part in the conversion ceremony of Shri/Shrimati _____ s.o./d.o. _____ resident of _____ from _____ religious faith to _____ religious faith do hereby, give intimation of the conversion as required by sub-section (1) of Section 5 of the Arunachal Freedom of Religion Act, 1978 (No.4 of 1978) as follows:-

1. Name of person converted _____
2. Name of Father of person converted _____
3. Address of the person converted in full
   Village _____
   Anchal _____
   Circle _____
   P. O. _____
   District _____
4. Age _____
5. Sex _____
6. Occupation and monthly income of the person converted _____
7. Whether married or unmarried _____
8. Name of persons, if any dependent upon the person converted _____
9. If a minor, name in full address of the guardian, if any _____
10. Whether belongs to the Scheduled Caste or Scheduled Tribe and if any so, particulars of such caste or tribe _____
11. Name of the place where the ceremony has taken place with full address:
    Place (village/town) _____
    Anchal _____
    Circle _____
    P. O. _____
    District _____
12. Date of conversion _____
13. Name of person who has performed the conversion ceremony and his address _____
14. Names of at least two persons other than the priest/or and the person giving intimation, present in the conversion ceremony _____

Signature of the religious priest the person taking part in the conversion Ceremony.

I, undersigned do hereby declare that what is stated above is true to the best of my knowledge and belief.

Date _____
Place _____

■ ■ ■

The Arunachal Pradesh Extraordinary Gazette,
September 12, 1979

FORM B
(See Rule 4)

Received intimation under Section 5 of the Arunachal Pradesh Freedom of Religion Act, 1978 (No.4 of 1978) on _____ from Shri/Smt. _____ with respect to the conversion of Shri/Smt. _____ s.o. /d.o. _____ resident of_____ from _____ religious faith to _____ religious faith.

Deputy Commissioner,
District _____

Dated _____

■ ■ ■

The Arunachal Pradesh Extraordinary Gazette,
September 12, 1979

FORM C
(See Rule 5)
Register of conversion

1. Name of the person converted _____
2. Father's name of the person converted _____
3. Address of the person converted in full
   House No._____
   Village/Town _____
   Anchal _____
   Circle _____
   P.O. _____
4. Age _____
5. Sex _____
6. Occupation and monthly income of the person converted _____
7. Whether married or unmarried _____
8. Name of persons, if any, dependent upon the person converted _____
9. If a minor, name and full address of the guardian, if any _____
10. Whether belongs to the Scheduled Caste or Scheduled Tribe and if so, particulars of such Caste or Tribe _____
11. Name of the place where the conversion ceremony has taken place with full detail
    House No. _____
    Village/Town _____
    Anchal _____
    Circle _____

P. O. _____
District _____
12. Date of conversion _____
13. Name of person who has performed the conversion ceremony and his full address _____
14. Name of at least two persons other than the Priest/the person giving intimation present at the conversion ceremony _____

■ ■ ■

The Arunachal Pradesh Extraordinary Gazette,
September 12, 1979

FORM D
(See rule 6)

Report for the month of _____
No. of intimation received during the month _____
Religion wise _____
Intimation
Breakup of the religion from which converted _____
Religion to which converted _____
No. of persecutions, if any, instituted under the Act _____
No. of acquittals and convictions under the Act during the month _____

                                        Deputy Commissioner (Negi)
D/S.   District _____

Deputy Secretary Law and Parliamentary
Arunachal Pradesh, Itanagar

8

UNIVERSAL DECLARATION OF HUMAN RIGHTS—ARTICLE 18

Everyone has the right to freedom of thought, conscience and religion; this right includes freedom to change his religion or belief, and freedom, either alone or in community with others and in public or private, to manifest his religion or belief in teaching, practice, worship and observance.

■ ■ ■

International Covenant on Civil and Political Rights—Article 18

1. Everyone shall have the right to freedom of thought, conscience and religion. This right hall includes freedom to have or to adopt a religion or belief of his choice, and freedom, either individually or in community with others and in public or private, to manifest his religion or belief in worship, observance, practice and teaching.

2. No one shall be subject to coercion which would impair his freedom to have or to adopt a religion or belief of his choice.
3. Freedom to manifest one's religion or beliefs may be subject only to such limitations as are prescribed by law and are necessary to protect public safety, order, health, or morals or the fundamental rights and freedoms of others.
4. The States Parties to the present Covenant undertake to have respect for the liberty of parents and, when applicable, legal guardians to ensure the religious and moral education of their children in conformity with their own convictions.

DOCUMENTS RELATED TO THE PERSECUTION OF CHRISTIANS

Document 1:

January 28, 1971

To
    The President of India
    Rashtrapati Bhavan
    New Delhi

Sub: Persecution of Christians in NEFA

Respected Sir:
I write on behalf of the Council of the Baptist Churches in North East India (CBCNEI) and also to express the feelings of the minority Christian community in North East India. My own church, the CBCNEI, is composed of about 2,20,000 communicant members in North East India with a total community of six lakhs.

Our church has been historically related to NEFA for many years now. It may be recalled that as early as the year 1840 the first book printed for the NEFA people was printed by the Baptist Mission in the Nocte Naga Language who are a people of the Tirap division of NEFA. At about the same time we maintained a mission station at Namsang in NEFA. More recently we have printed a literacy primer in Adi language and also some other books for the Adi people. Thus we have been in contact with NEFA people for more than 130 years now.

This past year my office has received appeals for help. I do not know all the details as it is impossible for my church to send people into the area to investigate. Thus, I base my comments on petition received by myself and from personal talks with various NEFA people.

I am led to believe that Government has taken a strong decision in the past one or two years to wipe out Christianity from NEFA and to threaten anyone thinking of becoming a Christian. I would hope my position is wrong, as a secular Government as we have in India, should not take any stand for or against any religious movement. But, I am burdened by the weight of the various petitions and talks I have had with NEFA people.

These people feel that Government has moved against them. Government has refused to protect them and their property, also refused to protect their places of worship and their sacred holy books. Government has threatened them and imprisoned, and in some cases have issued externment orders for them to leave their own homeland, for no other reason than that they have become Christians and/or they practice their Christian religion.

Under the circumstances I appeal to Government as follows:

That Government issues an immediate order to the various authorities in NEFA to stop any and all threats and acts of persecution against the Christian people of NEFA.

That Government takes immediate steps to safeguard the life and limb of the Christians in NEFA, our fellow citizens, and give them the same basic rights and privileges as any other citizen.

That Government appoints a special investigating committee composed of both Government leaders and leaders from the NE India Christian Council, to look into the allegations of persecution of the Christians in NEFA.

That some damage has been done to personal property of Christians or the property of church, under the very eyes of the Government officers, that Government grant compensation to repair the damage.

Please accept this prayer for help at your earliest convenience.

Yours humble servant
Sd/- K. Imotemjen Aie
Copy to: 9 authorities, General Secretary of Baptist Churches in North East India

Document 2:

Statement of Likha Alei, Son of Likha Riao
Suto village, Ziro Sub-division, Subansiri Dist., Arunachal Pradesh

On June 4, 1974 I was in my house with my family members. The following persons, viz. Tara Epo (High School student), Likha Taka (Gaonbura), Tao Tai, Likha Yakho, Tar Tazil, Likh Tadih, and Dabla Taram Likha Heri came to my house. Tara Epo caught me by the hand and started beating me right and left. Likha Yakho also joined in the beating till I became unconscious. When

I regained consciousness I found myself bleeding profusely from my cheek where I sustained a cut injury. I could not eat anything nor get up from my bed for three days. Afterwards I began to improve and I decided to come to Tezpur Mission Hospital for treatment on 22.6.74 and now I am feeling much better.

I am one of the leaders of our church. That is why I have been singled out for persecution. Although I have suffered pain, I shall not deny my faith in the Lord Jesus Christ.

Likha Alei
Suto Village, Ziro Subdivision
Subansiri Dist.

Document 3:

Date: 22.7.71

To
>The Member of Parliament
>For NEFA
>New Delhi

Sub: Entreaty for hearing

Sir,
With my due respect, I on behalf of my Tangsa people place under mentioned case before you, for your rightful justification and consideration of the case.

That Sir, on the 30th Dec 1970, the following people were arrested in connection with the sudden disappearance of Shri Bermey Tikhak. The arrested persons are as follows:

Sri Kamwang Chamchang
Sri Khiran Chamchang
Sri Mitching Murang
Sri Thakna Taikam
Sri Keyngi Murang

Shri Bermey Tikhak, disappeared in the year 1969, on March 8. These five people were arrested under suspicion of the disappearance of that man. But the administration had not yet found any clue of the murder of that lost man providing that these five persons are responsible for the murder.

Since they were arrested, it is now 7th month running without giving a hearing trial to the public. Under which law the administration is keeping these five people for such a long time in custody? If they are the culprits then there must be a public hearing trial which make the matter clear to the public that they are the culprits of the murder.

On the other hand, this man had business with them which are possible causes for ending his life. These people should also undergo a court trial. But it is grievous to see that the administration is keeping silent on the part of the associates of that man. This act of the administration has caused unpleasant idea about the administration in the hearts of the peace loving local people which may lead to feelings of bitterness in the hearts of local people regarding the administration in the near future.

Every one of peace loving people will feel this act of administration as an act of injustice according to the law. If the administration could have given a public hearing trial and proved that these five persons are murderers of the lost man, it is satisfactory to all the local people. Everyone will support that such criminals should get adequate punishment according to the law.

It is my earnest request that, you will take an immediate action in this matter.

Yours humble servant
Sd/- Longkhap (M. Yanger) Kimsing

Document 4:

Eastern Theological College
P. O. Rajbari
Jorhat, Assam
India

Date: 25.1.72

Dear brother,
What to do? Being a Christian, I have to face the problem which is too painful to hear. Without being guilty, I am being accused of having conspiracy with underground Nagas to murder Mr. Gora Pertin, who is the main leader of anti-Christian group in my area. So planned to have meeting on the 15th Jan., which was supposed to be attended by thousands of people from various divisions, but it was cancelled on account of Indira Gandhi's inauguration of Arunachal Pradesh on 20th Jan. So they said to me that it will again take place on Feb. 20. So again I have to go. Anyway my case been confirmed and Mr. G. Pertin told me that he found me not guilty and I need not be worried. But as many people heard and suspecting, I must be present. My case was made serious because of treasonable words of my friend Mr. ———. That is why, nowadays, I have no confidence in my brother — anyhow, anybody. Moreover, there is no proof of it. In this next meeting they will condemn Christianity and will accuse Mr. Lego for murder

case. They will charge him a sum of Rs.1000/- as fine because he is the President of Adi Church Council. This will also effect to Mr. Kuku Lego because he is the secretary of our church. The place meeting will be at Parbuk. They will also pass a resolution to burn down the remaining churches and to wipe out Christianity completely. Anyhow, let's see the mighty acts of God in this year.

Please do pray for this and for me so that God may help me to overcome evil and fearfulness.

In Subansiri Division, Nyishi student fellowship and church council meeting took place on 9-12 Jan. led by Mr. K. Tana.

Hope to receive your inspiring letter.

Your friend Yonthen Lego

* Rev. Yonthen Lego was the first Baptist Field Secretary among the Adi Baptist Christians.

Document 5:

Persecution of Christians in Arunachal Pradesh 1969-72
Churches Burnt

Name of the Place	Persecutor	District	Date
Magi village church	Dagmo Zini, C. O.	Siang	22.10.70
Dipa village church	"	"	26-28.10.70
Zipoo village church	"	"	29.10.70
Rach & Peri churches	J. S. Singh, E. A. C.	Subansiri	20.2.71
Thao village church	"	"	27.2.71
Depi village church	R. K. Patir, ADC	Siang	8.12.70
Apoo village church	J. S. Singh, EAC	Subansiri	1.3.71
Namoi village church	B. K. Gurung, DC	Tirap	18.11.71

Individuals

Jailed:
Kamwang, Mitchin, Khiran Dikey, Thakna and Kamlong were arrested by D. C., Tirap District, B. K. Gurung of (Arrested on 28.12.70, released on 28.1.71)

Beating up and other various treatments:
Smt. Lengbia Yopu beaten and stripped in public by Tasar Mangkha, cut with *dao* (blunt side) by D. C., Ziro, T. C. Hazarika. Hands and legs of Takam Han were tied up and kept 4 days without food in 1.1.72 by the same D. C. & Tasar Mangkha, *Zilla Parishad* member of Palin area.

Present situation:
Since the end of 1972, the complaints were lodged against the persecutors and the persecution to the central government. The last year has passed without much incidents, except verbal threat and some attempts to prevent the spread of Gospel by threatening fine and imprisonment, though opposition is still there even now.

Document 6:

The Persecution of 1974
(Our original document being very lengthy, only a summary is given below)

On 04.01.74, under orders from Tadar Tang, the churches of Khelim (East and West) were burnt.

On 19.03.74, Naharlagun church was burned at the order of Tadar Tang, Councillor.

On 15.04.74, a batch of students from Doimukh Govt. High School held a public meeting in Tarung Camp, Sagalee area, and incited the public to join in the harassment of Christians. On the same day these students and their followers went to Laptap village, burned the church and Christian houses, killed domestic animals and looted properties belonging to Christians.

On 16.04.74, the students and their followers went to Revi village and in spite of protest and pleadings from the Christians, they destroyed and looted all properties belonging to Christians and burned the church also. The students and their followers were armed with guns, bows and arrows, spears, clubs and *daos* and claimed that they received the authority for their lawless acts from the Chief Commissioner himself. Their leaders were:-

Tao Tania, student, Doimukh Government High School
Nabam Atum, student, Doimukh Government High School
Tarin Dapke, student, Doimukh Government High School
Tana Epo, *zilla parishad* member from Sagalee area

(Note: Doimukh Government School and the villages listed in this document are in the neighbourhood of Itanagar. Hence these things took place under the very nose of the administration and we summarise below the events of the following days.)

Churches were burnt, Christian homes were set on fire and Christian properties were looted by the same group.

Name of place	**Date**
Pang village church	17.04.74
Yalin village church	18.04.74
Socho village church	20.04.74
Karoi village church	20.04.74

Gotupu village church	23.04.74
Bobia village church	24.04.74
Lidi village church	24.04.74
Tabyi village church	24.04.74
Khat village church	26.04.74
Gai village church	28.04.74
Khil village church	02.05.74
Lekhi village church	02.05.74
Laptap village church	05.05.74
Pech village church	08.05.74
Depo village church	10.05.74
Grammaopop village church	11.05.74
Luru village church	14.05.74
Balizan village church	16.05.74
Cher village church	20.05.74
Pick village church	29.05.74

■ ■ ■

Names of Christians Who Have Been Assaulted in Various Villages

Tadar Taro, Nabum Takar, Kara Niya, Kara Khoda, Tana Ekha (later died), Techi Tagam, Techi Tegi, Techi Merchi, Techi Yelli, Techi Tamin, Teli Tad, Techi Rotu, Teli Yani, Nabam Hade, Nabam Tada, Teli Kam, Teli Tade, Takam Tela, Chera Saphung, Nabam Sakha, Nabam Sekho, Nabam Begi, Kara Tari, Nabam Tekhi, Nabam Tati, Nabam Tara, Nabam Kacho, Ngru Serbang, Deba Picha, Techi Chada, Techi Tabo, Techi Yam, Techi Taram, Techi Bagi, Techi Khep, Tala Tepi, Tai Yata, Taku Reja, Nabam Taso, Nabam Bagi, Nabam Tugung, Nabam Takam, Chukhu Serbang, Tara Tagi, Nabam Yaga,

Techi Taji, Taba Nake, Taba Nam, Nabam Nikhi, Techi Epo, Tayam Sampi.

■ ■ ■

The Teli Ekhu Story and Subsequent Events

On 11.07.74, Teli Ekhu, wife of Teli Tad of Khemli village was beaten up by Teli Guma of Khemli village on the orders of B. Kumar, Extra Assistant Commissioner (EAC), Sagalee area because she refused to renounce her Christian religion. This woman then went to North Lakhimpur, Assam and reported it to the Nyishi Christian leaders who have taken refuge there. On hearing this B. Kumar became angrier and sent for Teli Ekhu. On 20.07.74, Teli Ekhu appeared before B. Kumar, EAC in his office. Kumar then ordered Techi Teki, a zilla parishad member, to strip her naked before the public, and after this she was kept hanging upside down from her feet for 36 hours during which no one was allowed to give her anything to eat. While she was in this position, Techi Teki poked her private parts with a stick and asked everybody to observe the spectacle. Later, Kumar told Techi Teki that he could keep the woman as servant. So he is keeping her in his house on the orders of the EAC. (As destiny would have it. It was Rev. Fr. C. C. Jose who pulled him out from his accident vehicle from a spot just above the mandir on Naharlagun-Itanagar road. I believe he apologised to Fr. Jose for the hateful and harmful things he did to Christians of Arunachal Pradesh. Fr. Jose took him to hospital and Takar Techi died of multiple complications.)

On 15.08.74, B. Kumar sent for Nabum Boki of Bobya village. When he appeared in the office of the EAC, B. Kumar ordered Techi Teki to abuse Nabum Boki for refusing to renounce his Christian faith. At this, Techi Teki caught hold of Nabum Boki by the knot of his hair and dragged him around, which is a great insult according to the Nyishi custom.

On 18.08.74, when Techi Tulo and Techi Tara of Karoi village appeared before the EAC by the order they were asked to retract the statement they had given to the Christian leaders about the loss they suffered from the hands of the persecutors. When the two men refused to oblige, Kumar ordered them to be hung by their hands for 11 hours. Later, both were asked to put their thumb impressions on a paper whose content they did not know, after which they were allowed to return to their village. The men who tortured these two on the orders of Kumar are Techi Takar and Techi Dodum. Techi Tulo and Techi Tara were also fined two mithuns worth Rs. 1,000 each.

On 21.08.74, Nyair Jil of Khat village was beaten by Techi Teki on the order of Kumar for refusing to retract his report to the Nyishi Christian leaders about the loss of his property at the hands of the persecutors. He was forcibly made to put his thumb impression to a statement saying that what he had reported was false. Nyair Jil maintains that he had lost much more than he had reported.

On 23.08.74, Nabum Tara and his wife Nabum Sai of Khat village were summoned by Kumar to his office. When the poor man appeared with his wife before the EAC, he was asked to retract his report of the loss he had suffered at the hands of the persecutors and also to deny his Christian faith. On his failure to do so, the EAC fined Nabum Tara one mithun for disobeying him. Further, Nabum Sai was kept in the EAC's office as a security till he produced the mithun as fine.

■ ■ ■

For the sake of brevity, we will cut short the narration and draw some conclusions.

The following extracts are also taken from the original document.

■ ■ ■

Conclusions

The atrocities committed on Christians as described above clearly shows that this was a well planned movement directed against the Christians of Subansiri District in pursuance of the resolutions adopted at the public meeting in Ziro on 15.7.72. The fact that the government authorities did not take any precautionary measures to prevent such lawless activities, and that such activities were allowed to continue for more than a month under their very noses is clear proof of the collusion of the government authorities in the harassment of Christians in the Subansiri District of Arunachal Pradesh.

There is also evidence to prove the complicity of government officials in the harassment of Christians particularly in Sagalee area. All of this gives a lie to the claim that India is a secular state. When the rights of minorities are trampled underfoot, and where murder, arson and looting are condoned because the victims happen to be Christians, it is sheer hypocrisy to claim that all religions are equal in the eyes of the state.

It is also a known fact that Tadar Tang, Councillor for Subansiri District, who holds a position analogous to a Minister of State, has been distributing large sums of money to the groups of students who were engaged in the harassment of Christians as narrated above. From what source and for what purpose Tadar Tang got the money is anybody's guess. The very fact that a person holding the position of a Minister of State could actively participate openly in the harassment of Christians without let or hindrance, is beyond comprehension. The only conclusion one can arrive at from all of this is that the Arunachal Pradesh Territory Administration is determined to stamp out Christianity from the face of the territory. The question is, will the Government of India allow this to happen?

* These facts were published jointly in 1980, by Rev. L. M. Yanger, Secretary of Arunachal Christian Action Committee and the Chairman of ACAC.

Document 7:

Tana Ekha, the First Christian Martyr in Arunachal Pradesh

Tana Ekha, son of Tana Sera of Sango village, in Sagalee subdivision of Subansiri District, aged about 45 years, was a Christian leader of good standing. He was a wealthy man by his own tribal standards and a respected leader of the community.

On 25th April, 1974, some students of Doimukh Government High School, viz., Techi Dodum, son of Techi Tade; Nabum Ekha, son Nabum Pade of Tabi village; Nabum Khamia, son of Late Nabum Tade of Tabi village and others, came to Sango vil-lage and went to the house of Tana Ekha. They demanded of Tana Ekha that he renounce his Christian religion. On his refusal to do so he was beaten up and kicked around till he was bleed-ing from his nose and mouth. Then he was lifted up and thrown down from his house to the ground with the result that his stool came out with blood. Then his house was set on fire and burned down to ashes.

Tana Ekha was then taken to the Doimukh Government Hospital, but he was refused treatment there because he was Christian. He finally died on the sixth day after he was beaten up, on 1.5.74.

By refusing to deny his faith, Tana Ekha paid the supreme price with life. May he be an example to those who are following in his footsteps. Let us remember, "The blood of the martyr is the seed of the church."

* *AIM Magazine*, October 1974 Vol. No.10. *AIM Magazine* is published by the Evangelical Fellowship of India.

Document 8:

UNION TERRITORY OF ARUNACHAL PRADESH
OFFICE OF THE CIRCLE OFFICER
NAMPONG: TIRAP DISTRICT

No. NPC-51
        Date:- Nampong the 12th day of May 1975

To
  Sri Maikam Tikhak, Honkap village
  Sri Waching Tikhak "
  Sri Ngatkam Tikhak "

A complaint has been received from the people of Taipong, Kovin and Honkap that you are indulging in such activities which go against the principles of local culture and faith and thereby creating disturbances of peace among villagers.

You are hereby directed to report in my office on 14.5.75 failing which force may be used to compel your presence.

(C. Bordoloi)
Circle Officer

Nampong

Memo No. NPC-51 Dated, Nampong the 12th day of May 1975
Copy to:- Sri Watang Samai, Member, Tirap Zilla Parishad, Honkap. He is also requested to come to discuss about the matter. It is understood 2 or 3 families more are going to accept a new culture and faith in a day or two. This may please be stopped.

(C. Bordoloi)
Circle Officer
Nampong

Document 9:

GOVERNMENT OF ARUNACHAL PRADESH
OFFICE OF THE DEPUTY COMMISSIONER: SUBANSIRI DISTRICT: ZIRO

ORDER

Memo. No. C. 2790/75/27

Dated Ziro the 11th Dec '75

This is for general information of all that prior permission of the Government of Arunachal Pradesh is required before any place of worship such as churches, temples and mosques is made failing which action will be taken to demolish them as unauthorized buildings.

Permission is, however, not required for building of houses of traditional worship, such as DONIPOLO EUGYANG.

Gaon boras, etc, are requested to give wide publicity to this order with their villages.

Sd/- (J. M. Syiem)
Deputy Commissioner
Subansiri District, Ziro

Memo. No. C.2790/75/27

Dated Ziro, the 11th Dec 1975

Copy to:-
All GB's in Subansiri District.
The Executive Engineer, Ziro.
The Asstt. Executive Engineer, Doimukh
The Asstt. Engineer, Ziro.
The D. C. IO SIB, Ziro
Notice Board

For wide circulation in their office
Sd:- 11/12/75
Deputy Commissioner
Subansiri District, Ziro

Document 10:

GOVERNMENT OF ARUNACHAL PRADESH
OFFICE OF THE DEPUTY COMMISSIONER
SUBANSIRI DISTRICT: ZIRO

NO. C. 2790/75

Dated Ziro, the 28th Jan 1976

With reference to his petition dated 22nd Jan. 1976, Shri Likha Tapu of Ambam village is hereby informed that no permission can be given for construction of Church in his village. He has been explained personally about this today.

Sd/- (J. M. Syiem)
Deputy Commissioner Subansiri District: Ziro

Date:- 28/1/76

Shri Likha Tapu,
Ambam village,
Ziro II.

Copy to:-
The GB of Ambam village, Ziro II, for necessary action.
Sd/- (J. M. Syiem)
Deputy Commissioner
Subansiri District: Ziro

Document 11:

OFFICE OF THE CIRCLE OFFICER: PALIN CIRCLE GOVT. OF ARUNACHAL PRADESH MEMORANDUM

It has come to my knowledge that in spite of the instruction contained in the Deputy Commissioner, Ziro order No. C.2790/75/27 dated 12.12.75 issued to all Panchayat Leaders and GB's of this Circle, some people of Rakso, Redang and Cholo are contemplating to erect a church at Rakso village violating the above order of the Deputy Commissioner, Ziro. It is also learnt that this type of activities are resulting in some social discontentment among some section of people of the said village. Some influential leaders of these three villages are, therefore, asked hereby to instruct those concerning section of people not to erect any church or demolish if any such building has since been constructed.

Sd/- (M. Ray Hajong)
Circle Officer Palin

Memo. No. PA/CON-1/37-47
            Dated Palin, the 24th Dec '76

Copy to;-
Shri Dobo Tayang, Ex-ASM, Rakso.
" Byabang Mangha, GB, Rakso.
" Dari Kagi, GPM, Rakso
" Bril Kame, ASM, Rakso
" Byabang Taro, GB, Radeng
" Byabang Heri, GPM, Radeng.
" Byabang Rui, Radeng
" Takem Kha, GB, Cholo
" Takem Laniang, GPM, Cholo
" Byabang Bangso, Rakso
" Byabang Taro, GB, Rakso
For wide publication and compliance

Date:- 24/12/76
            Sd/- CIRCLE OFFICER PALIN
                SUBANSIRI, DISTRICT

Document 12:

GOVERNMENT OF ARUANACHAL PRADESH
OFFICE OF THE ASSISTANT
COMMISSIONER: MIAO

NO.FOR/CASE/77/14763-65

Dated Miao, the 25th Feb '77

To,
    Shri Mokan Kimching, GB, Songking village
    Shri Terrong Longphi, Retired PI, Songking village
    Shri Longkhap Kimching, Songking village

Reports received that you have encroached Forest Land far away from your village at a distance of one and a half km and starting clearing jungles and making buildings in deep jungles to settle some villagers with the intention to acquire Government Forest Land without the specific order from the competent authority. You should be aware of the fact that this kind of occupation is highly illegal and you should restrain yourselves from such illegal activities.

You are hereby directed to stop such illegal activities of clearing jungles and constructing buildings. In case you have those immediately and vacate the area completely. The vacation report of the area must be submitted to the undersigned within 7 days on receipt of the letter, failing which legal action will be taken against you.

Sd/- EAC, Miao

Document 13:

OFFICE OF THE DEPUTY COMMISSIONER
GOVT. OF ARUNACHAL PRADESH
TIRAP DISTT. : KHONSA

NO. CA. 24/77

Dated Khonsa, the 15th March '77

To,
    Shri Longkhap Merang Yanger
    Executive Secretary
    Tirap Baptist Churches Council

Sir,

It has come to notice that you are thinking of constructing a church near Sonking village of this district.

You are hereby informed that no church/temple, etc. can be constructed without prior permission of the government.

If any church/temple is constructed without the permission of the government it will be demolished.

Kindly acknowledge receipt of this letter.

Yours faithfully
Sd/-   (Smt. Vineeta Rai)
Addl. Deputy Commissioner
Tirap Dist., Khonsa

Document 14:

To,
   The Deputy Commissioner, Khonsa
   Arunachal Pradesh

Sub: To take necessary action before 31st August 1978 for the resolution against Christians.

Sir,
We the Wancho Baptist Association state the following for your kind and necessary immediate action.
   That the anti-Christian activities are going on against the Christian minority at Mopaghat village in Kanubari area.
   A public meeting was held at Kanubari camp on 20th August 1978. The meeting led by the area public leaders and Rajas, and they have resolved that all Christians from Mopaghat must leave their home before 31st August 1978, otherwise their houses will be burnt down and will take action against Christians.
   We therefore request your honour to give protection to save us from these anti-Christian activities.
   We honour the Indian constitution and want to live with all people in peace. We have nothing to do against other religions.
   Therefore we request your honour to act without delay in order to avoid troubles between the Christians and the non-Christians.

Yours faithfully,
Wancho Baptist Church Council
Dated 24th August 1978

Document 15:

GOVT. OF ARUNACHAL PRADESH LIEUTENANT GOVERNOR'S SECRETARIATE, ITANAGAR

No. LG 11/77 (Part 11)
                                Date, Itanagar the 5th October, 1978

From:
  Shri T. P. Khaund
  Secretary to the Lt. Governor
  Itanagar

To:
  The Secretary
  Supply and Transport, Govt. AP
  Shillong

Sub: - Release of cement from public sale quota

Sir,
I am directed to enclose herewith a copy of an application from Shri Samchom Ngemu, General Secretary, Tangsa Singpho Cultural Society, P. O. Namchik, Tirap Dist. Arunachal Pradesh about release of 600 bags of cement required for a Buddhist temple at Kharsang.

2. The Buddhist temple at Kharsang is very important project and has to be completed expeditiously. I am, therefore, directed to request you kindly to instruct the Deputy Commissioner, Tirap

district, Khonsa to release 600 bags of cement from public sale quota to the Tangsa Singpho Cultural Society as early as possible.

Encl. as above.

Yours faithfully,
Sd/- T. P. Khaund
SECRETARY

Memo. No. LG. 11/77 (Part11)
Copy to: -

Dt. Itanagar the 5th Oct. '78

1. The Deputy Commissioner, Tirap District, Khonsa along with a copy application from the General Secretary, Tangsa-Singpho Cultural Society for information. He is requested kindly to arrange 600 bags of cement to the society for construction of a proposed Buddhist temple at Kharsang.
2. Shri Samchom Ngemu, General Secretary, Tangsa-Singpho Cultural Society, P. O. Namchik Kharsang, Tirap District for information.

Sd/- T. P. Khaund SECRETARY

Document 16:

GOVT. OF ARUNACHAL PRADESH
OFFICE OF THE EXTRA ASSIST. COMMISSIONER
TIRAP DISTRICT: MIAO

NO. N/CON-7/75-78/442-45

                        Dated, Miao, the 5th Nov. '78

To
    The GB
    The Secretary, (TBCC), Songking

Sir,
Enclosed please find herewith the copy of office memo NO. CA /24/78/43 date.16-10-78 from the Deputy Commissioner, Khonsa for favour of your information and strict compliance.

Yours faithfully,
Sd/- B. Baruah 5/11
Extra Asst. Commissioner Miao

■ ■ ■

GOVERNMENT OF ARUNACHAL PRADESH
OFFICE OF THE DEPUTY COMMISSIONER
TIRAP DISTRICT: KHONSA

No. CA. 24/78/43

                        Dated Khonsa the 16th Oct '78

This is for general information of all concerned that no house of worship, other than those in respect of the traditional faith, will be allowed to be constructed thereafter without the prior permission of the Government.

If such houses of worship are constructed without Government's permission they will be demolished without any liability to the Government.

Sd/- J. M. Syiem
Deputy Commissioner
Tirap District: Khonsa

■ ■ ■

URGENT
GOVERNMENT OF ARUNACHAL PRADESH
OFFICE OF THE EXTRA ASSISTANT
COMMISSIONER: MIAO

No: M/CON-7/75-78/12268

Miao the 22nd November'78

NOTICE

It is to remind you that construction of any religious temple/church other than those of indigenous faiths has strictly been prohibited as per order of the Deputy Commissioner, Khonsa which was forwarded to you vide this office letter No. M/CON-7/75/467-39 dated 25/10/78. It is learnt from reliable sources that one church is being constructed in your village. Please ensure that no construction of any church/temple be taken up in your village and if any structure has, meanwhile, been erected, the same should be immediately demolished as per order of the Deputy Commissioner, Khonsa. A copy of the letter No. CA-24/78/43 dated 16th Oct'78 received from the Deputy Commissioner, Khonsa is also enclosed herewith again for your immediate compliance.

Please confirm action taken on the matter failing which necessary action will be taken as per law.

Enclo: as stated

Sd/- B. Baruah 22/11/78
Extra Assistant Commissioner
Miao Sub-Division: Miao

To
    The G.B.
    Songking Village

Document 17:

To,
    The Executive Engineer
    Capital Project Civil Division No. (1)
    CPWD Itanagar. Doimukh Camp
    Arunachal Pradesh

Sub: List of Contractors of Sagalee-Doimukh Truckable road

Sir,
I have the honour to submit the list for the Sagalee-Doimukh truckable road to you. You are requested to distribute the road

side according to the list of contractors and you kindly adjust them in the road side.

The Christian contractors should not be provided road work as they are foreign agents, because they are getting money from foreign aid. Such anti-nation or anti-social activities should not get any business within Arunachal Pradesh, according to the Fundamental Rights Act 1978. Because they are supplying the India government's activities to the following members were sent to Shillong and Nagaland to report against the Govt. of Arunachal Pradesh to foreign government from 8.11.78 and returned on 19.11.78.

(14 names are given)

Above mentioned Contractors should not provide Roadside Work or other business as they are anti-nation leaders)

(78 names are suggested for the work)

The following given members are selected for the action committee. They are requested to conduct the contractors when work will be distributed in the road sites. If the contractors will disturb or create trouble to the engineers, the action committee members will solve the problems. The names of the members are furnished below.

(10 names are given)

Yours faithfully,
Sd/- (Takar Techi)
Chairman, Sagalee-Doimukh
Social Welfare Convention
Itanagar (A. P.)

Copy to:
To all ministers of A. P. for your kind information

The Chief Secretary, the Secretary L. G., the E. A. C.
The Circle Officer, Doimukh for kind information.
The Assistant Engineer, Doimukh Sub-division to kindly mention above information.

Takar Techi
Chairman, Doimukh-Sagalee
Social Welfare Convention
Itanagar, A. P.

Document 18:

The Secretary,
Minority Commission,
Government of India
19, Willington Crescent,
New Delhi—110 001.

Sub: Prayer for redress of grievances of the Christian Community in Arunachal Pradesh

Sir,
On behalf of the Christians of Arunachal Pradesh, we beg to submit the following for favour of your kind consideration and action:

From the very beginning Christians had to face opposition and hardships from their own tribal communities. In spite of this, the number of Christians kept increasing and is still increasing even now.

In January 1969, the opposition to Christianity took a violent turn in Subansiri District when their churches in Den, Deed and Neelam villages were burnt down on the orders of a Government official. This violent opposition to Christianity became more and more widespread with the active connivance of the Arunachal Pradesh administration and finally culminated in the burning down of over 40 Churches and large scale destruction and looting of Christian property in April/May, 1974 as a result of which over 2,000 Christians were rendered homeless and they had to seek shelter in the jungle for months together.

These violent acts against Christians and their property were reported both to the local administration and the Government of India by the people themselves as well as by the North-East India Christian Council and the National Christian Council including representatives of the Arunachal Pradesh Christians who waited on the Prime Minister and Home Minister of India in June and December, 1974. In the memorandum submitted to the Prime Minister (copy enclosed) a prayer was made for safeguarding the life and property of Christians and for ensuring religious freedom in Arunachal Pradesh. We regret, however to say that these representations fell on deaf ears.

Although there was no large-scale violence against Christians from 1975 to 1977 there had been a covert threat held out against Christians, who were prohibited by Government order to rebuild their churches destroyed in 1974 disturbances (copy enclosed) and prohibited to meet for religious worship even in private homes. Christian government officials were warned by the authorities to refrain from holding religious worship service in their homes on pain of disciplinary action.

In May 1978, the Arunachal Pradesh Legislative Assembly enacted the infamous Freedom of Indigenous Faith Bill, now renamed as Freedom of Religion Bill, which has now received the assent of the President of India in the face of massive opposition from all parts of India.

After the above mentioned Bill was passed in the Arunachal Pradesh Legislative Assembly, the Chief Minister of Arunachal Pradesh made a speech on the floor of the house (copy enclosed) in which he outlined the proposed Government action against those who forsook their ancestral faith which, we understand, is being implemented now.

While the controversy was raging whether or not the President should give his assent to the Indigenous Faith Bill, a memorandum was submitted to the President of India threatening violence against Christians beginning from January 1979. This has given rise to widespread apprehension among Christians that large scale violence against Christians similar to the one in 1974 will erupt in the first week of January 1979 unless the Government takes immediate action to prevent such occurrence. As our past appeals to the local government and to the Government of India for protection of our lives and property had been consistently ignored, we find no alternative but to appeal to you to do all you can to save us from the atrocities and indignities we suffered in 1974 from the hands of hoodlums who appear to enjoy the protection of the powers that be.

There had been also instances of discriminations against Christians in matters of employment and promotion in the government which can be unearthed and proved only through an impartial investigation and inquiry.

Because of all that had happened in the past as we have narrated above, the Christians in Arunachal Pradesh feel that they are worse than second class citizens in their own land and that they are being treated more like criminals than law-abiding citizens. There is a feeling of insecurity and fear in their own minds which is now aggravated by the enactment of the above mentioned notorious Freedom of Religion Bill.

Our request is that the Minority Commission would take up our cause immediately with the Government of India and compel them to take immediate action to redress our long standing grievances and also ensure the safety of our lives and property.

We are enclosing herewith all the documents we have earlier submitted to the Government in the past along with other documents relevant to this position.

We trust that you would be good enough to take immediate action on the lines we have indicated above.

We remain,
Yours faithfully,

Sd/- Taram Neelam
President, Subansiri Baptist Convention
C/O J. N. College, Pasighat
Siang District, Arunachal Pradesh

Sd/- T. Ering
    Secretary
    Siang Baptist Association

D. Bhuyan
Executive Secretary
North Bank Baptist Christian Association
P. O. Charali, Darang District
Assam

Dr. L. C. Rema
Field Coordinator
Baptist General Conference North Bank Mission
Tezpur, Assam

Document 19:

Members of National Christian Council of India

The National Christian Council of India
and Heads of Churches
Nagpur—440 001

24th March, 1979

Dear Friends,
Representatives of the Catholic Bishops Conference of India and the National Christian Council of India met in Delhi on March 22nd, to consider appropriate steps to be taken by the CBCI and the NCCI in regard to the Arunachal Freedom of Religion Act 1978.

The joint meeting,
Resolved that:

i) A writ petition be filed in the Supreme Court of India jointly by the CBCI and the NCCI challenging the validity of the said Act;
ii) Further advice be solicited from other jurists in order to strengthen the case further before approaching the Supreme Court;
iii) The CBCI and the NCCI Secretaries be authorized to take the necessary steps for implementing the above decision.
iv) The Supreme Court be urged to reopen its earlier decision upholding similar Acts of Madhya Pradesh and Orissa.

To implement this decision it was decided in the joint meeting to appoint a Central Action Committee of three representatives each from the CBCI and the NCCI which should meet at the earliest possible to plan strategy and action .

It has also been decided to:

i) Promote state wise action committees jointly of Roman Catholics, Protestants, Orthodox and others to plan and execute appropriate action at state and local levels.
ii) Place a petition before the Minorities Commission to look into the harassment and discrimination against Christians as a result of the implementation of Arunachal Freedom of Religion Act.
iii) Mobilize and enlist the support of Christians in all states, especially in states where Christians are in substantial numbers,
iv) Galvanizing the support of people of other faiths who are supporters of democracy and secularity.
v) To observe at an appropriate time a day of prayer and fasting by all Christians in the country as a mark of protest against the said Act.

A petition has been signed by all who attended the joint meeting and submitted to the Speaker of the Lok Sabha stating objections to the Freedom of Religion Act.

The joint group:

a) Endorsed the appeal issued earlier by the CBCI to observe Friday, April 6th, 1979 as a day of Prayer and Fasting, and intercession on behalf of the Nation.
b) Appeals to every Christian individual, family and congregation to contribute generously to:

i) Help Arunachal Christians.
ii) Meet cost of the Supreme Court appeal.

The National Christian Council of India appeals to every diocese, Annual Conference, Synod, Mandalum, congregation, family and individual:

1. To observe April 6, 1979 as a day of Prayer and Fasting and to remember especially the protagonists of the Freedom of Religion Acts and Bill because they need Christian love and forgiveness as much as we do.
2. To wait prayerfully for guidance from the Central Action Committee for the day of prayer and fasting as mark of protest, which will be observed some weeks later.
3. To contribute generously and send your contribution to the National Christian Council of India, Nagpur, M. S. 440 001.
4. To pray for:
    i) The NCCI – CBCI Central Action Committee;
    ii) The Governments concerned, Indian Parliament and Central Ministers;
    iii) Arunachal Christians; and
    iv) Neighbours who profess other faiths but who also are children of the same Father in heaven.

Your Servant and His,

Sd/- M. A. Z. Rolston
General Secretary

Dear Friends,

You are requested to immediately implement these recommendations, particularly, the day of prayer and fasting on April 6/1979. It would most apt if a 24 hour chain of prayer is conducted on this date beginning from 12 midnight to 12 midnight.

Bounded in His Service.
(P. B. M. Basaiawmoit)

Secretary,
North East India Christian Council,
Dinam Hall, Jaiaw, Shillong – 793002

Document 20:

CATHOLIC ASSOCIATION OF BENGAL

3, Lenin Sarani,
Calcutta 700 013

THE GREAT RALLY AND MARCH ON SUNDAY,
MARCH 25TH, 1979
P R O G R A M E

Commencing at 2:15 pm, at Park Circus Maidan
    Bengali Hymn led by Fr. A. Mitra, S. J. and Choir
    Opening Prayer by His Eminence Cardinal L. T. Picachy, S. J., Archbishop of Calcutta.
    Introduction by Mr. L. G. Stuart, President, Catholic Association of Bengal

"Discrimination and atrocities meted out to Christians in Arunachal Pradesh"
Speaker—Mr. Wanglat Lowangcha

Hymn in English

"Freedom of Religion Bill"
Speaker—Mr. G. S. Reddy, M.P.

"Freedom of Religion Bill" (in Bengali)
Speaker—Mr. Joseph Gomes

Reading of Memorandum in English and in Bengali

Comments and vote of thanks
    Mr. Neil O' Brien, M. L. A.

Procession leaves Park Circus Maidan for Raj Bhavan to present the Memorandum to His Excellency the Governor of West Bengal

■ ■ ■

THE SPEECH OF MR. WANGLAT LOWANGCHA, GENERAL SECRETARY OF THE PEOPLE'S PARTY OF ARUNACHAL ON 25th MARCH 1979

Ladies and Gentlemen,

On August 15, 1947 India won her Independence. What has Independence meant to Arunachal Pradesh? Has it meant freedom for the people of the North-Eastern Frontier? Or, has it meant a new type of colonialism, by which the freedom-loving people of this Union Territory will forever continue to be told what to do, what to think, what to choose, whom to vote for, what religion to follow?

The first election in Arunachal Pradesh was held thirty years after Independence. Who ruled us till then? A Chief Commissioner who wielded greater powers than a colonial officer in the heyday of colonialism.

I do not like to describe the way the last elections were held in Arunachal Pradesh – the restrictions on the Opposition, the manipulation of votes, the intimidation used, the full exploitation of the ignorance of the people—I will briefly put it this way: today's puppet regime in Arunachal Pradesh is the creation of Shri K. A. A. Raja and an appointed cabinet which behaves much like school boys before the Lt. Governor, who in turn waits for the next instruction from the Home Ministry, Delhi. The democratic processes have been reversed: the people are told what to do. All thinking, planning and deciding takes place above; and orders descend to the people through a well-graded hierarchy of sycophants.

Let me now come to the point. We are "told" that our culture is beautiful, our traditions great, our heritage an unsurpassable wealth. We know that already, there is no need for these self-appointed guardians of our culture, these interfering exponents of our traditions to tell us that. We are "told" that the religion of our ancestors is respectable; we know that too, and no one will show greater respect to various religious traditions than we people of Arunachal.

But we are freedom-loving people. We want to be free and we respect the freedom of others. We do not want to be accountable to the DC when we accept any religion of our choice. The Freedom of Religion Act has taken away this freedom. We do not like to be called up by some authorities and asked why we are marrying a Christian girl, or sending a son to a Christian School, or taking a trip to Shillong or Kohima.

You will ask: have these things happened? Can such things happen in Independent India? Not these only, there are worse things to tell you. It all began with the avowed intention of helping us to preserve our culture. But what was done was to make a determined bid to impose Hinduism on us. Temples were erected at government expense, Hindu mission schools and other institutions were opened at state cost, and pilgrimages to Hindu shrines were subsidized.

At the same time not even the least Christian influence was allowed to penetrate the Union Territory. No Christian priest or preacher was allowed entry, it was forbidden to put up Christian churches, erect Christian schools. What was worse, children who took admission in Christian schools would be called back and sent for re-education to some (Rama Krishna Mission) Hindu School. We have the greatest respect for our Hindu friends and their beautiful institutions, but we want our freedom of choice respected.

Christianity is not a new religion in Arunachal Pradesh. In the 1830s the American Baptists opened a mission in Namsang (Tirap Dt.). In the 1850s Fathers Krick and Bourry worked among the Adis and Nyishis. Long before Independence there were small Christian communities in Arunachal Pradesh. But the arrival of Independence meant the loss of religious freedom in the Union Territory. Bibles had to be underground, biblical extracts were copied and passed around. Churches could not be erected, public worship was forbidden, Christian education for Christian children rendered impossible. However without the help of any outside missionary, Christianity spread from man to man, from home to home. The very restrictions imposed brought the beautiful religion of Christ and drew more people to it, and the Arunachal administration grew alarmed at the rapid growth of the Christian community in spite of the "Iron Curtain" that hung at the borders of the Union Territory. In villages where Christians were numerous, small bamboo-and-thatch churches began coming up to the deep dismay of the Arunachal authorities. In some places they got these demolished by bribing, harassing and threatening in turn. In other places they followed the "Divide and Rule" policy. They made use of the organizations for the promotion of culture and student welfare to raid the Christian villages, beat up the Christians, put to fire the churches, loot and burn their houses and rob their domestic animals. What had taken place intermittently from independence, took place on a vast scale in 1974. In most of these villages people have not dared to put up churches since then.

Injured people remained bed-ridden for months, and the homeless lived in the jungles for about a year. Even these cruel measures did not seem to discourage people from becoming Christians. Not one apostatized; vast numbers chose to join the persecuted and accept baptism. It was under these circumstances that the genius of our Lt. Governor devised the Freedom Of Religion Bill, which took away all our freedom. When the whole world was celebrating the Human Rights Year, Arunachal authorities passed a bill for suppressing some of the basic human rights of any human being. And though the whole nation protested against it, it received the President's assent, and the Chief Minister announced that the bill had unanimous support of all the thinking sections of India. Thus became law a set of rules, of which any civilized country would be ashamed.

A person who changes his religion has to report to the DC. And who is the DC to question the genuineness of my conversion? How am I obliged to give account to a secular officer the reasons for my personal religious choices? How is he competent to judge, when he belongs neither to the religion I have abandoned nor to the one I have accepted?

If, even before such a bill was passed, the Arunachal authorities could have had recourse to active persecution; what an effective tool they now have for persecuting the Christians. Reports are reaching us of arrests and of anti-Christian activities. Now that an anti-conversion bill has been introduced in the Parliament, what is our guarantee that what happened in Arunachal Pradesh will not be repeated on a larger scale all over the country? Many have felt that the events in Arunachal Pradesh were but a dress-rehearsal for monstrous designs for the nation.

There are some standing who may still doubt whether all these things have taken place, whether such things can take place in Independent India. I would invite you to come over and meet the victims (that is if you succeed to penetrate the Iron Curtain). If there is a priest here, let him try to get a pass from the Arunachal Government to enter the Union Territory and meet his fellow-Christians. We hope he will not get the answer the Bishop of Tezpur got, when he was refused permission to give the consolation of religion to his Christians on the occasion of Christmas. We have heard of such refusals only at the hands of totalitarian and the atheistic regimes, ––– and from the Arunachal Administration. Fellow Christians of Calcutta, obtain from our Government the permission to erect churches, open Christian schools and hospitals, to live a fuller Christian life like you and millions of Christians in this country and elsewhere do.

Today we ask that the Freedom of Religion Bill introduced in the Parliament be withdrawn. Not only that, we want that the acts already in force in Arunachal Pradesh, Madhya Pradesh and Orissa should be repealed. We further demand that all discrimination against Christians, against Christians of scheduled castes, against Christian priests and preachers, against Christian institutions and activities —— and every other form of discrimination be speedily ended. Finally, we demand that a firm guarantee be given to the minorities that the constitutional safeguards will be respected. We owe allegiance to a secular India, not to Hindustan or the leadership of a few fanatics. We can call on all the Christians, we urge all minorities, we appeal to the enlightened sections of the minority community to lend us your support in our struggle for freedom. We shall not rest until we have won it, won the WHOLE OF IT.

Jai Hind.

L. Wanglat, Calcutta
Date: 25.03.79

(This was reported in *Telegraph* and *Amrita Bazar Patrika* in March 1979 from Kolkata. On hearing this, Chief Minister P. K. Thungon moved a "calling attention motion" for discussion in the Arunachal Pradesh Assembly during the Budget Session of 1979. A resolution was moved condemning my speech.)

■ ■ ■

Statement of Chief Minister P. K. Thungon on the Calling Attention Notice regarding news item captioned "Christians Protest Rally" appearing in a section of newspapers of March 26, 1979, and the statements reported to have been made by the General Secretary of the People's Party of Arunachal.

The attention of the Government has been drawn to the news item which appeared in a section of newspapers on 26th March, 1979, under the caption "Christians Protest Rally."

The Government has no information whether any local Government official had persuaded Shri Wanglat Lowangcha not to marry a girl of another faith. This is a personal matter and the fact remains that Shri Wanglat Lowangcha did marry a girl of another faith.

The allegation that instigated by Government officials, some people had stripped naked the wife of Shri Taniang because she would not give up Christianity and that she was hung upside down is absolutely false and baseless. Perhaps Shri Wanglat Lowangcha refers to the alleged maltreatment meted out to Smt. Teli Ekhu in 1974. In a memorandum dated 12.9.74 submitted to the Prime Minister of India, Shri Nabum Rukhi, President, Nyishi Baptist Association had, inter alia, made an allegation that Smt. Teli Ekhu, wife of Shri Teli Tad of Khemly village in Sagalee Sub-division was publicly stripped naked in full public view on the orders of EAC, Sagalee and was kept hanging upside down for one day and one night in the EAC's office premises for the simple reason that she refused to renounce her Christian faith. The then Chief Commissioner ordered high level official inquiry into the alleged incident. The Enquiry Committee was headed by the then Chief Secretary.

The Committee had taken the statements of a number of people including that of Smt. Teli Ekhu herself in the presence of her husband after making it clear to her that she should tell the truth without any fear or apprehension. Apart from denying the allegation, she deposed that she had never met or seen the EAC nor did she know whether he was "black or white." On being asked whether anybody else apart from EAC insulted her or ill treated her, she replied in the negative. She also denied having made any complaint to Shri Nabum Rukhi, President, and Nishi Baptist Association. She stated that nobody had ever caused any injury to her or her husband. The Committee came to the conclusion from the evidence given by various persons that Smt. Teli had never been called to the office of EAC, Sagalee, and that she had not been subjected to any maltreatment. In the report, the Committee also made the following observations:-

> It would, therefore, appear from the above that the numerous allegations received by the Administration are by and large fabricated and grossly exaggerated. They appear to be the product of a highly imaginative and mischievous mind (minds) that are determined to malign the tribal people and the local administration. In this regard it will be worthwhile mentioning that Shri Nabum Rukhi now reported to be staying at North Lakhimpur Mission Compound are all illiterate. Shri Nabum Rukhi can just write his name in Roman script. The petition purported to have been sent by him appears to be the creation of some persons working behind him and using his name.

During the course of their visit, the local people asked the Committee about the purpose of enquiry and wanted to know who had made such wild allegations. The enquiry led the local people to believe that some undesirable elements were making false allegations against their conduct. During their talks with the Committee, the elders urged before the Committee that such falsehood must be checked and if the Government did not do anything, they would be compelled to take action according to their customs.

It is also false to say that 40 churches were burnt down at the instance of Government officials. No church whatsoever has been destroyed at the instance of any Government official and instead of making wild and sweeping statements, it would have been appreciated if any specific case had been brought to the notice of the Government. We have information about demolition of one or two churches by the people themselves voluntarily, for example, recently in Changlang circle; a group of Tangsas who voluntarily embraced back traditional Tangsa faith demolished themselves their own church.

The last elections were free and fair and it is mischievous to say, at this stage, that Christians were not allowed to freely persuade the voters. In the election, Shri Wanglat who himself was a candidate and who got defeated, should have filed an election petition if he had faith and belief in the rule of law. In fact, the statement of Shri Wanglat Lowangcha shows that perhaps he himself was trying to persuade the voters to vote for him by invoking religious statements which is an unfair practice. Furthermore, the allegation of Shri Wanglat Lowangcha that Government officials decide what religion a man will practice is malicious and false.

The Government of Arunachal Pradesh would welcome the Central Government to satisfy themselves whether there is even an iota of truth in the allegations of Shri Wanglat Lowangcha and take appropriate action for preventing such spread of falsehood which disturbs harmony and peace.

The Arunachal Pradesh Freedom of Religion Act 1978 was a legislation passed by this house and assented to by the President. The intention behind the legislation has been made amply clear before the house. It is not the voluntary acceptance of a faith or religion that is being prevented; what the legislation prohibits is only conversion from one religion to another by force or fraud or inducement.

The reported statement of Shri Wanglat Lowangcha has already agitated the minds of the Honourable Members of this House and other leaders and I understand that a number of local leaders have issued a statement condemning Shri Wanglat Lowangcha's statement.

A statement of the type made by Shri Wanglat Lowangcha leads us to believe that there is some design by interested quarters to malign the Government and the people of Arunachal Pradesh and to mislead the people in other parts of the country as well as outside the country.

■ ■ ■

THE VICAR GENERAL
ARCHBISHOP'S HOUSE
32, PARK STREET,
CALCUTTA—700 016
TELEPHONE—44-1960

REF. NO. 672/1979/C-1(a)

March 26, 1979

Mr. Wanglat Lowangcha,
Meghalaya House,
Calcutta.

Dear Mr. Lowangcha,
On behalf of the Archdiocese of Calcutta, I thank you for coming up here and speaking at our rally and taking part in our procession. Your speech did much to enlighten us on the events in Arunachal Pradesh. We are only sorry that nothing was done all

these years. However, let us not look back past but to the future, trusting in God's Grace for guidance and courage.

May God bless you and your people in your struggle for justice. Please convey my thanks to your companions.

Yours sincerely

(Alan de Lastic)
VICAR GENERAL

■ ■ ■

Memorandum presented by the Catholic Association of Bengal to his Excellency the Governor of West Bengal

Your Excellency,
We, the Catholic Association of Bengal, representing the Roman Catholic citizens of West Bengal and Christians throughout India, united with us, respectfully invite your Excellency's attention to the following:

We are Christians, Indians and loyal citizens. As such, we have rights not inferior to those of any other citizen.

We have served and will continue to serve our country. In the fields of medical, educational and social service, our contribution has been greater than our numbers warrant. These services have been rendered to all our fellow citizens, irrespective of caste, creed or religion, and no charge of any ulterior motive has ever been laid at our doors. Yet, in Arunachal Pradesh, our rights have been blatantly violated. Our places of worship have been desecrated and destroyed; our fellow Christians have been attacked and discriminated against. Our brothers and sisters in that part of the country can only practice their religion in fear and trembling.

Article 25 of our glorious Constitution permits anyone to profess, practice and propagate the religion of his choice and freely spread its tenets. Yet the so called "Freedom of Religion Act," recently passed by the Arunachal Pradesh Assembly and the parallel Bill introduced into the Lok Sabha, are not intended to prevent conversions by force, fraud or inducement as they pretend, but are really intended in their operation, to prevent any conversions at all by introducing a reign of Police Raj in the sphere of religion. As a consequence these Bills prevent the free exercise of the rights guaranteed to all religions under Article 25 of the Constitution of India.

Why should any citizen not have the right to adopt and practice the religion of his choice without reporting his choice to any Government Official?

What right has the Government to monitor personal expressions of conscience? Why should any citizen be hindered from becoming a Christian or embracing any other religion?

The Catholic Church "forbids forcing anyone to embrace the faith, or alluring or enticing people by unworthy techniques. By the same token, she also strongly insists on a person's right not to be deterred from the faith by unjust vexations on the part of others" (Vatican Council II, Decree on the Church's Missionary Activity No.13).

Why should any Government pretend that Christian Missionaries act otherwise than in accordance with the principles of their own religion?

Accordingly we demand:-

> That the iniquitous Freedom of Religion Act in Arunachal Pradesh be immediately repealed.

That the proposed Freedom of Religion Bill be not considered or re-introduced in the Lok Sabha. That a parliamentary commission including Christian members of the Lok Sabha be set up immediately to investigate the injustices being inflicted on the Christians in Arunachal Pradesh, so that justice and freedom may be restored to them without delay.

We therefore, request and urge you, as the Constitutional Head of the State of West Bengal, to forward this petition to the Governor of Arunachal Pradesh, and to the President of India.

Sd /-
Mr. L. G. STUART
President
CATHOLIC ASSOCIATION OF BENGAL
3, Lenin Sarani,
Calcutta—700 013.

Date: 25th March, 1979

Document 21:

54 Lower Circular Road,
Calcutta—16

25th March, 1979

An Open Letter of Mother Teresa of Calcutta to Mr. Morarji Desai, Prime Minister of India, and the Members of the Indian Parliament, regarding the Freedom of Religion Bill 1978.

Dear Mr. Desai and Members of our Parliament,
After much prayer and sacrifices I write to you asking you to face God in prayer, before you take the step which will destroy the joy and the freedom of our people.

Our people as you know better than I—are God-fearing people. In whatever way you approach them—in presence of God—the fear of God is there. Today all over the country everybody feels insecure because the very life of freedom of conscience is being touched.

Religion is not something that you and I can touch. Religion is the worship of God—therefore, a matter of conscience. I alone must decide for myself and you for yourself, what we choose. For me the religion I live and use to worship God is the Catholic religion. For me this is my very life, my joy and the greatest gift of God in His love to me. He could have given me no greater gift.

I love my people very much, more than myself, and so naturally I would wish to give them the joy of possessing this treasure, but it is not mine to give, nor can I force it on anyone. So also no man, no law, no Government has the right to prevent me nor force me, nor anyone, if I choose to embrace the religion that gives me peace, joy, love.

I was told that Gandhiji had said: "If the Christians would live their lives according to the teaching of Jesus Christ there would be no Hindus left in India." You cannot give what you do not have.

This new move that is being brought before the Parliament under the cover of freedom of religion is false. There is no freedom, if a person is not free to choose according to his or her conscience. Our people in Arunachal are so disturbed. All these years our people have lived together in peace. Now religion is used as a deadly weapon to destroy the love they had for each other, just because some are Christians, some Hindus, and some tribals. Are you not afraid of God?

You can call Him: ISHWAR, some call Him: ALLAH, some simply God, but we all have to acknowledge that if HE who made us for greater things; to love and to be loved, who are we to prevent our people to find this God who has made them—who loves them—to whom they have to return.

You took over your sacred duty in the name of God—acknowledge God's supreme right over our country and her people. It was so beautiful. But now I am afraid of you, I am afraid for our people. Abortion being allowed has brought so much hatred—for if a mother can murder her own child, what is left for others to kill each other. You do not know what abortion has done and is doing to our people. There is so much immorality, so many broken homes, and so much mental disturbance because of the murder of the innocent unborn child in the conscience of the mother. You don't know how much evil is spreading everywhere. Mr. Desai, you are so close to meeting God face to face. I wonder what answer you will give for allowing the destruction of the life of the unborn child, and destroying the freedom to serve God, according to one's choice and belief. At the hour of death, I believe we will be judged according to the words of Jesus who said:

> "I was hungry, you gave Me food
> I was thirsty, you gave Me to drink
> I was homeless, you took Me in
> I was naked, you clothed Me
> I was sick, you took care of Me
> I was in prison, you visited Me.
>
> Truly I say to you, for as long as you did it to these the least of my brothers, you did it to Me."

> Gandhiji has also said: "He who serves the poor serves God."

I spend hours and hours in serving the sick and the dying, the unwanted, the unloved, the lepers, the mental,—because I love God and I believe His words: "You did it to me." This is the only reason and the joy of my life: to love and serve Him in the distressing disguise of the poor, the unwanted, the hungry, the thirsty, the naked, the homeless and naturally, in doing so, I proclaim His love and compassion for each one of my suffering brothers and sisters.

Mr. Desai and Members of Parliament, in the name of God, do not destroy the freedom our country and people have had, to serve and love God according to their conscience and belief. Do not belittle our Hindu religion saying that our Hindu poor people give up their religion for a "plate of rice." To my knowledge, I have not seen this being done, though we feed thousands of poor of all caste and creed, though thousands have died in our hands beautifully in peace with God.

I remember, I picked up a destitute man from the street who was nearly eaten up with maggots. He said gratefully: "I have lived like an animal in the street, but I am going to die like an angel, loved and cared for." And he died a beautiful death, loved and cared and in peace with God.

I have always made it my rule to cooperate whole-heartedly with the Central and State Governments in all undertakings which are for the good of our people.

You will be glad to know that we are cooperating very earnestly in helping in family limitation through morally sound means. In Calcutta alone we have 102 centres where families are taught self-control out of love. Here we promote the moral, legal and scientific method of Natural Family Planning. From 1971 to 1978, we helped 11,701 Hindu families, 5,568 Muslims and 4,341 Christian families. Through this natural and beautiful method there have been 61,397 less babies born.

Turning to another sad point, I wish to inform you that I have been trying to get into Arunachal Pradesh for some time now, but so far I have not succeeded and yet Ramakrishna Mission members are entering freely. We are in 87 places in India. Why are we not with our poor in Arunachal?

I pray and I beg to you that you order a day of prayer throughout the country. The Catholics of our country have called an all-India day of fast, prayer and sacrifice on Friday, 6th April, to maintain peace and communal harmony and to ensure that India lives up to its tradition of religious freedom. I request you to propose a similar day of intercession for all communities of our country—that we may obtain peace, unity and love; that we become one heart, full of love and so become the sunshine of God's love, the hope of eternal happiness and the burning flame of God's love and compassion, in our families, our country and in the world.

God bless you.

(Sd) M. Teresa M. C.

Document 22:

CATHOLIC UNION OF INDIA

2nd April, 1979

Hon. Shri Morarji Desai
Prime Minister of India
New Delhi

Dear Prime Minister,
I have a dual responsibility in writing to you. First of all on behalf of 13 million Catholics in this country whom I honour to represent and secondly, as the only Janata M. L. C. in the State.

Christians all over the country are bitter and frustrated for many reasons. A systematic and well calculated attempt is being made to interfere in the legitimate minority rights of the Christian community.

The support of the Janata Government to the Freedom of Religion Bill of Mr. O. P. Tyagi is causing grave concern to all of us. Christians have every right to profess, practice and propagate their religion and this Bill is particularly aimed to destroy this function and curb all Missionary activities in the future. The existing panel provisions of the land are sufficient; punish conversions brought about by force, fraud or inducement. Why then this Bill? In this connection, I welcome your assurance to Archbishop Pimenta that this Bill will not be accepted as it is and that you are willing to discuss these matter in detail with the representative of the Church Laity.

Another matter of grave concern to the community is in regard to the plight and suffering of Christians in Arunachal

Pradesh and Bihar. Reports reaching us speak of burning and desecration of churches and acts of hooliganism and violence against priests, nuns and laity. I must also mention the murder of Catholic priests in Bihar as also the recent attack on a convert in Bihar.

Added to all these is the discrimination practiced against Harijan converts to Christianity and less of side and concessions to this section of people. Over 60 lakhs of people suffer such discrimination all over the country and this problem cannot be wished away just because you as Prime Minister cannot see eye to eye with us on this issue.

There appears to be a growing anti-Christian bias in some States and in certain quarters and the erosion of genuine religious freedom. I do not wish to accuse you of such bias but it is up to you to assuage the feelings of the Community and to put down all acts of violence and persecution with a firm hand.

I must draw your attention to the Janata Party Manifesto of 1977 and request you to take all steps necessary to honour the commitment to Christian Minorities.

I would very much appreciate a reply if possible so that any action oriented programme planned by the church and laity may be deferred.

Thanking you,

Yours sincerely

(D. V. D'Monte) MLC
National President

Document 23:

MEMORANDUM SUBMITTED TO THE HON'BLE CHIEF MINISTER OF ARUNACHAL PRADESH BY THE CHRISTIAN COMMUNITY OF THE TERRITORY

Respected Sir,
We the Christian community of Arunachal Pradesh is very proud of being a part of this great land of India. India has won her Independence thirty years ago. The Constitution of this land has granted every citizen right of equal liberty, law in social and economic justice, freedom of expression of thought, belief, faith and worship.

By the virtue of our heritage of citizenship of this land, we are loyal citizens to the state in every aspect of our lives. In spite of this, we are being defamed and maliced publicly by the Government of Arunachal Pradesh by giving defamatory names and titles, such as "foreign elements," "foreign agents," "anti-national," "anti-social," "anti-cultural" and so on. And thus we are being levelled with the common criminals.

After making us common criminals, we are being given "right" punishment, such as physical imprisonment, mental and psychological torture by threats of life imprisonment and threats of death punishments. We are also being discriminated in social, political, economic, education and religious life. Our property has been taken away and churches destroyed. We are being socially excommunicated.

All these "right" punishments are being given to us for a plain and simple reason—our faith in Jesus Christ! This faith transforms our inner lives. This is being expressed by giving up certain evil elements of social and cultural practices such as nature worship which is based on human fear of all natural gods—such as the god of a mountain, god of a river, the god of the family, the spirit of death and so on. We have been worshipping these vain gods from our forefathers' time. By worshipping these gods we are constantly in the bondage of insecurity and fear of displeasing these gods. Thus our lives have been in the bondage of fear and uncertainty.

Our traditional culture is based on our beliefs. So we have many cultural and social practices which are by nature evil, wasteful, and unsuitable for this rapidly changing modern age. For example, head-hunting (which was the crown of our forefathers' culture), communal feud, polygamy, burying the dead underneath the house, infanticide of twins, rejecting a paddy field when a lightning strikes, slaughtering of slaves and so on. The Christian community is reforming these evil social and cultural elements by accepting Christ and allowing the Divine Power to reform and elevate our lives. This Divine Power transforms the believer's inner lives in getting rid of drunkenness, vice, immorality along with the above cited evil elements.

The government is also doing the same reformation work of social and cultural upliftment. But the method being used by the government is different—human machineries. By the use of force, fraud, inducement and bribery. Why triple financial facilities are being provided to the students who are studying in the R. K. Mission Schools in comparison to the students studying in other schools, colleges and universities? The government is encouraging certain people by giving highest financial facilities and other provisions to persecute the Christians and to stop those who are willing to become Christians and use force to Christians to deny their faith. Is it not use of force, fraud, inducement and bribery?

Therefore, we the Christian community of Arunachal Pradesh plea very humbly but very firmly and strongly to the government of Arunachal Pradesh and the Central government for the following actions:

> Immediate repeal of the "Freedom of Religion Act".
> Full restoration of our fundamental Rights which have been denied.
> Compensation for the churches destroyed and for those who have been physically imprisoned.
> A strong protest against the proposed Central Anti-conversion Bill.
> May God give you wisdom to take action according to His Will

Yours faithfully,

On behalf of the Arunachal Christians

L. M. Yanger,
Executive Secretary,
Tirap Baptist Church Council

2nd April, 1979

Document 24:

To,
> The Chief Secretary,
> Government of Arunachal Pradesh,
> Itanagar.
> Subject: Inner Line Permit

Sir,
I will be grateful to you if you will kindly issue Inner line Pass to Rt. Rev. Joseph Mittathany, D. D., Bishop of Tezpur, Assam and Rev. Fr. Cherian Moolamattam, Vicar General, Bishop House, Tezpur, Assam to visit Itanagar along with the Member of Parliament. Their purpose of visit to Itanagar will be to meet the Hon'ble Lt. Governor and the Chief Minister of Arunachal Pradesh. Inner Line Permit may please be issued for a period of one month from 4th April '79 in my care of.

With thanks

Yours Faithfully,

Dated: Itanagar
The 3rd April '79

(Wanglat Lowangcha)
General Secretary of PPA,
Camp Itanagar, A. P.

Document 25:

NORTH-EASTERN INDIAN CHRISTIAN ACTION COMMITTEE: SHILLONG UNIT
C/O. NEICC OFFICE, DINAM HALL, JAIAW, SHILLONG- 793 002

4th April 1979

To,

Sub: Black flag Demonstration.

Dear Friend,

Greetings:
You are perhaps very much aware of the imminent opposition against practicing the basic tenets of the Christian faith and the whole of India is actively thrown into action oriented programmes of demonstrating and battling against this unsecularistic and undemocratic curtailment of religious freedom.

In recent years, two Religious Freedom Bills became Acts and consequently upheld by the Supreme Court in January 27, 1977. Then last year, Arunachal Pradesh adopted its Freedom of Religion Act and the last blow came on December 22, 1978 when O. P. Tyagi introduced a Bill in the Parliament called "Freedom of Religion Bill, 1978" (No.178 of 1978)! The Prime Minister, in a recent interview in Bombay, said that the same Bill will not be passed; instead another Bill of the same name will be passed in the immediate future. However, we are in jeopardy if any Bill (whatever the wording may be) is passed by Parliament to curb religious freedom.

Therefore as a mark of protest, we call upon all Christians in Shillong and around, irrespective of your denominational background to join in a black flag demonstration on SATURDAY APRIL 7, 1979.

The Prime Minister of India will be arriving in Shillong for the NEHU Convocation at about 11:30 am and we would like for you to begin proceeding from your respective places from 10:00 am onward to fill up the entire spectators column on the Prime Ministers route to the Convocation Hall. The line up should start from Lum Mawbah junction and as far as possible, right up to the Civil Hospital via Additional Secretariat to Raj Bhavan.

It is not only hundreds that should demonstrate but thousands and the whole Christian population, young and old, men and women. Further, it should be silent in a meditative atmosphere and solemn hymns could be sung during the occasion. It is advisable that you arrange in congregations and sacrifice your time, prestige, etc., for the sake of Christ.

In addition to your black flags, please prepare as many placard as possible of varying sizes and slogans but clear and visible with the following captions/slogans.

LET GOVERNMENT NOT INTERFERE WITH RELIGION
RELIGION IS THE PREROGATIVE OF THE DIVINE NOT OF THE HUMAN
ANY FREEDOM OF RELIGION BILL WILL CAUSE FANATICISM

ANY FREEDOM OF RELIGION BILL DESTROYS
FREEDOM
ANY FREEDOM OF RELIGION BILL DESTROYS
DEMOCRACY & SECULARISM
ANY FREEDOM OF RELIGION BILL IS
ANTI-CHRISTIAN

DEAR MORARJI
DO NOT EQUATE YOURSELF WITH THE NEROS,
THE HITLERS,THE PHARAOHS AND OTHER
FANATICS.
WELCOME TO THE HILLS
BUT
PLEASE DROP FREEDOM OF RELIGION BILL
BECAUSE
IT DESTROYS DEMOCRACY AND SECULARISM

You are requested to prepare at least 8 placards, each bearing a slogan as indicated above. Above the slogan, you could add a sign of the Cross in red colour.

This is a last minute arrangement but your cooperation and involvement in the eleventh hour is extremely necessary.

With best wishes,

Yours bonded in His labour,

Sd/-

1. (P. B. M. Basaiawmoit)
2. Rev. Fr. S. Sngi Lyngdoh, S.D.B

Document 26:

JOINT MEETING OF THE CATHOLIC BISHOP'S COUNCIL OF N. E. REGION AND THE REPRESENTATIVES OF THE CHRISTIAN CHURCHES OF N. E. INDIA, SHILLONG—5TH April, 1979, starting at 9:00 am.

AGENDA

Election of chairman and Secretaries

Bible Reading and Prayer—Rev. Gilbert Marak

Report of Delhi Meeting of Christian Leaders on March 25 1979—Bishop Denzil D'Souza

Arunachal Pradesh after passing of the Freedom of Religion Bill—Mr. Wanglat

Discussion on the joint-action to be taken by the churches in N. E. Region, in the light of the Arunachal Bill and the Central Bill on Freedom of Religion introduced in Lok Sabha on 22 December, 1978—Mr. Desai is to visit Shillong on 7th April, 1979, some representation is to be made to him.

Formulation of Message, Letter and Resolutions

Concluding words

PRAYER

■ ■ ■

MINUTES

JOINT MEETING OF THE CATHOLIC BISHOPS' COUNCIL OF N. E. REGION

AND

THE REPRESENTATIVES OF THE CHRISTIAN CHURCHES OF N. E. INDIA

Archbishop's House: Shillong
April 5, 1979

1. Election of Chairman and Secretaries :
    a. Archbishop H. D'Rosario of Shillong-Gauhati Archdiocese and Bishop D. D. Pradhan of Assam Diocese (CNI) were elected co-chairmen.
    b. Rev. Fr. M. C. Thomas (Rector of Don Bosco, Shillong) and Pre-Pastor P. B. M. Basaiawmoit (Secretary-North-East India Christian Council) were elected Secretaries.
2. Bible Reading and Prayers:
    Rev. Gilbert Marak of Tura read the Scripture and led in prayer.
3. Report of Delhi meeting of Christian leaders on March 22, 1979:
    - Mr. P. B. M. Basaiawmoit read out the resolutions adopted by the CBCI-NCCI Consultation and further added that the Churches in Mizoram, Manipur and Nagaland are everyday to render all cooperation necessary.
    - Concerning the day of prayer and fast on April 6 '79, he informed that as far as possible, Churches in Aizawl, Tura, Imphal, and Kohima and Shillong have

been contacted on the matter. However, as an alternative it has been proposed, we all of N. E. India can hold together a day of prayer and fast or wait an information from the Central Action Committee.
- Bishop D'Souza then further highlighted on the meeting held at Delhi since he himself was present. He added that it was further decided at the Delhi meeting that facts have to be collected and circulated in Parliament and State Legislatures in order that they may be enlightened of the true picture prevailing situation in Arunachal Pradesh.
- It was felt that public support should be galvanized in the best possible way- we should get non-Christians of like-mindedness to join the ACTION COMMITTEE, for what we can do together, should not be done separately.
- The Arunachal Act was also studied at the Delhi meeting and it was also felt that representatives from all over India should go to Delhi, and arrange a procession and present a memorandum to the Speaker of the Lok Sabha, praying for withdrawal of the tabled Freedom of Religion Bill, 1978.
- In connection with the Calcutta Rally of March 25, 1979, Bishop D'Souza informed the Shillong Consultation that it was arranged by the Catholic Association of W. Bengal

Mr. P. B. M. Basaiawmoit informed the consultation that an ad hoc Committee of three members was hurriedly formed for staging a black flag welcome to the Prime Minister on the stated day. However, permission is awaited.

Discussion on the joint-action to be taken by the Churches in the N. E. Region, in the light of the Arunachal Act and the Private Members Bill on Freedom of Religion introduced in the Lok Sabha on December 22, 1978.

The Christian leaders of N. E. India gathered together in the Archbishop's House, Shillong on April 5, 1979 wish to take place on record the following:-

1. The Freedom of Religion Bill now before the Parliament takes away a citizen's freedom of conscience,
2. The Arunachal Pradesh Freedom of Religion Bill has been much abused,
3. Contrary to the statement of Mr. H. M. Patel in the Lok Sabha, the Christians in Arunachal Pradesh have been harassed by the official machinery,
4. Three people have been arrested in the Changlang area (Tirap Dist.) of Arunachal Pradesh because of their belief in Christ; they were released only after they renounced Christianity under compulsion,
5. The Christians in the Salang village of the same area were terrorized into demolishing their own church,
6. During the last ten years more than 40 churches were put to fire,
7. The harassment of Christians continues; threats, intimidation, physical torture – every unfair means is used to terrorize the Christians,
8. Christian leaders are refused permission to visit their brethren in Arunachal Pradesh,
9. The Christians are forbidden to erect church buildings,
10. The Christians are forbidden to open educational institutions of their choice,

11. There is discrimination in the allotting of stipends to Christian students.

Formulation of Message, Letter and Resolutions:
Resolved that:

- A memorandum should be presented to the Prime Minister on the occasion of his visit to Shillong for the Convocation of NEHU.
- An appeal be sent out in the name of the participants to Christians throughout the country explaining the situation and asking for assistance.
- A publicity Committee be set up to give the maximum publicity to events in Arunachal Pradesh. The members selected were Rev. L. Lalthanmawia, Rev. Fr. Sngi Lyngdoh and the two Secretaries.
- Adequate information be provided to MLAs in various states and MPs who are Christians, so that they can help the Christian cause.
- At least one legal case be fought in the Guwahati High Court by an aggrieved Christian in Arunachal Pradesh, after due consultations with lawyers.
- A general *hartal* be observed on May 3 all over the North-East India in protest against the Freedom of Religion Bill and the harassment of Christians in Arunachal Pradesh.
- Support to be given to the black-flag reception to be accorded to the Prime Minister.
- An appeal be sent out to all Churches (even those not to be presented in the assembly) to join hands together against a common danger.

- A demand be made for the institution of an all party, all faith parliament committee to investigate the allegations of harassment of Christians in Arunachal Pradesh.
- Collection of funds be organized at various levels by all the Churches to defray the expenses involved in the work of publicity, legal action, organizational work, etc.
- The Human Rights Commission be approached with regard to the injustices committed against Christians in Arunachal Pradesh.
- A march to Itanagar be organized by our Christian brothers in Arunachal Pradesh.
- Application be made for the Inner Line Permit by various Church leaders (even if refused), in order to pile up evidence of discrimination.
- Similarly permission be sought for building of Churches in AP, for the same reason.
- Pamphlets be prepared for the people of Arunachal Pradesh answering the usual accusations against Christianity.
- Joint Action Committee be set up to follow the decisions. The members are:- the two co-chairmen, the two Secretaries, the Treasurer, the Revds. K. I. Aier, W. Manners, Canon, H. B. Sungoh, Dr. M. P. John, Dr. C. Lal Rema, Bishop K. Mittathany, Bishop D. D'Souza, Messrs. J. D. Pehrmen, H. Hadem, F. Lyngdoh, S. D. D. Nicholas-Roy, Rev. Dr. C. L. Hminga, Rev. Rokhuma, Rev. Fr. S. Sngi Lyngdoh and Mr. M. S. Jahrin.

Sd/- Secretaries:
(P. B. M. Basaiawmoit)
(Rev. Fr. M. C. Thomas)

■ ■ ■

JOTTINGS AND REMINISCENCES OF THE PRESS CONFERENCE GIVEN BY SHRI MORAJI DESAI, THE PRIME MINISTER OF INDIA, TO THE JOURNALISTS AND EDITORS OF SHILLONG ON THE 7TH APRIL 1979.[CE22]

On the 7th of April at 3:45 p.m., Shri Morarji Desai met the journalists and editors of Shillong in Raj Bhavan for a press conference. Many and varied were the topics discussed on that day. Three of these topics impressed the editor of the *Sur Shipara* very much: the black flag demonstration, the proposed Freedom of Religion Bill, and the imposition of Hindi on tribal students who would like to take the IAS, IPS, and IFS examination.

I. The Black Flag Demonstration
One of the journalists asked the prime minister what was his reaction to the black flag demonstration as organized by the N. E. I. Regional Joint Christian Action Committee. Shri Morarji Desai replied, "No flags and no stones can make me change my opinions if I think they are correct." At this point, the editor of the *Sur Shipara* intervened, though his words probably were not heard by the prime minister since there were two or three talking together, but he said, "It was not against your person, but against the wicked Freedom of Religion Bill."

II. The Proposed Freedom of Religion Bill
Another journalist put this question to the prime minister, "What do you think of the Christians opposition to the Freedom of Religion Bill?"

To this question, the prime minister answered thus:

Shri Morarji Desai: We shall not accept as it is. We shall change it.

Fr. Sngi: Will you change it in substance or only in words?

Shri Morarji Desai: No fundamental right of anyone will be curtailed. All are free to embrace the religion of their choice. But no one should force another to change his religion. (Evidently, Shri Morarji Desai has not understood and will never understand that conversion is the work of God alone . . . . This is a real pity.)

Fr. Sngi: We hope you will change it substantially. As it is now, the Bill is very wicked. Let us see what the new draft of this Bill will be.

III. On the Imposition of Hindi
Mr. B. Lanong, the Editor of the *U Lum Shyllong* asked the prime minister this question, "What about the imposition of Hindi on tribals for the IAS, IPS and IFS examinations?"

Shri Morarji Desai: We have seen to that. We have given them one year to learn Hindi.

Fr. Sngi: Mr. Prime Minister, one year is too short. It is impossible to learn well a language in one year in order to be able to write and express oneself clearly and forcefully.

Shri Morarji Desai: It is possible to learn it in one year.

Fr. Sngi: I would challenge anyone to do such a feat.

Shri Morarji Desai: You don't want to learn it.

Fr. Sngi: We want to learn it and we love it. But we need time. Kindly give us some 50 years to learn well.

Shri Morarji Desai: Then you go out of India, if you cannot learn it.

Fr. Sngi: Mr. Morarji Desai, Hindi is not absolutely one of the constitutive elements of "BEING AN INDIAN!" To be an Indian I have to be born of Indians in India. And I am so.

Shri Morarji Desai: How old are you?

Fr. Sngi: Nearing 60.

Shri Morarji Desai: And you have not learnt it!

Fr. Sngi: When I was a student, we had no possibility of learning it. Then even after Independence, the method of teaching Hindi has been horrible, to say the least. Instead of attracting people, it has actually repelled them. At this rate we shall not make much headway.

■ ■ ■

Freedom of Religion Bill Not to Be Withdrawn
In Shillong, an inter-denominational delegation of Christian leaders headed by Archbishop D'Rosario was given to understand by the prime minister on April 7 that the Freedom of Religion Bill now before the Parliament would go through substantially as it was.

The delegation approached through Sri Morarji Desai to submit to him a memorandum, when he was in Shillong for the convocation of the North-Eastern Hill University. The memorandum had been prepared by the church leaders of various denominations in North-East India who had met in the Archbishop's House, Shillong, on April 5.

When the delegation requested the prime minister to arrange for the withdrawal of the Freedom of Religion Bill now before the Parliament, he answered curtly: "It will not be done." When they urged him to arrange for the repeal of the Arunachal Pradesh Freedom of Religion Bill which had been much abused, his answer was equally firm and negative. He refused even to consider instituting an impartial inquiry into the allegations of harassment of Christians of Arunachal Pradesh. He said that the allegations were baseless and the accounts brought forward made up.

When it was brought to his notice that selective restrictions were imposed on the entry of Christians into Arunachal Pradesh, he promised to look into the matter. However, when the delegation complained about restrictions on the building of churches and opening of Christian educational institutions in Arunachal Pradesh, he showed evident annoyance, but promised to examine the issue.

Sri Morarji condemned the use of force and inducement in bringing about conversions. He said he strongly objected to the conversion of minors, of poor people in famine conditions. "This is not the way to increase Christian numbers," he stated emphatically. When the delegation asked him to cite even a single case of forced conversion, he asked in a loud voice, "Why should I bring it to you or to your Bishop? I will punish him. I will punish the guilty person."

Earlier in the day, in answer to a call from Christian youth groups, a large crowd of people had lined up all along the reception route and waved black flags to the prime minister as he was arriving. Breaking the usual tradition of cordial welcome to all visitors, Shillong had gone out to protest against the Freedom of Religion Bill and the harassment of Christians in Arunachal Pradesh.

Subsequently, a spokesman of the Christian community said that the joint action committee set up by the Christian leaders had called for a general hartal to be observed all over North-East India on May 3.

Document 27:

10th of April, 1979

To,
  The President of India,
  New Delhi
  Through the Congress AICC Study Team.

Sub: Arunachal Pradesh Freedom of Religion Act 1978 and persecution met by the Christians in Arunachal.

Sir,
We, the undersigned of the Arunachal Christian Action Committee, are deeply concerned about the manner and the unusual haste by which the Arunachal Pradesh Freedom of Religion Bill received the President's assent in spite of strong protest from the people of Arunachal Student's Communities including the post-graduates, the legislators of the opposition party. Since the enactment of this Bill, three people have been arrested in Tirap District under Section 3 of the Act, one Church has been pulled down in the Changlang circle and one Church has been burnt in Mopaghat area, two ploughing bulls have been confiscated and one pig has been killed and one cane chair destroyed on 26th March 1979 belonging to a Wancho Christian namely Sri Aram of Mopaghat. The above mentioned incidents are the examples of the atrocities met by Arunachal Christians. We have enough reasons to fear that legalized atrocities and persecutions might terrorize the sensitive zero of our country. We also believe that the government is using its administrative machineries to demoralize the Christians of

Arunachal Pradesh by their activities to destroy the rights and properties of Arunachal Christians.

The process of persecutions are not only of recent events but it has been enforced since 1969, e.g. on 7.1.69, Deed, Dem, Neelam and Saya Churches in Ziro area were burnt by the members of the home-guard on the orders of Sri Harban Singh, a home-guard commander. It was reported to D. C. of Ziro but he refused to take any action.

On 23.1.71, Sri Jagir Singh, the present E. A. C. (Sr.) Roing, ordered Lowant Wang, V. L. W. to assault Talo Sakha of Tarso village for no reason except that he is Christian.

On 6.2.72, Sri Tasar Mangha assaulted Byabian Ringcho because he was a Christian. On the same day Sri Mangha stripped naked Smt. Leggbia Yapu in public for refusing to renounce Christianity. The matter was brought before Deputy Commissioner but the Deputy Commissioner refused to take notice and dismissed the matter without taking any action.

On 19.3.74, Naharlagun Church was burnt on the order of Tadar Tang, the present Supply and Transport Minister of Arunachal Pradesh. His accomplices are Sri Techi Takar, Zilla Parishad member, Thana Epo and Techi Dodum. It may be noted that Naharlagun is at the outskirts of Itanagar, the new Capital of Arunachal Pradesh.

The above mentioned cases are some of the few atrocities met by the unfortunate Christians of Arunachal Pradesh.

Persecution to the Christians is still continuing.

We therefore earnestly request you: -

1) To remove the selective restrictions that have been imposed on the entry of Christians into Arunachal Pradesh,

2) To remove the restrictions on the building of churches for the Christians of Arunachal Pradesh,
3) To repeal the Arunachal Pradesh Freedom of Religion Act,
4) To withdraw the Freedom of Religion Bill now before the Parliament,
5) Immediately to institute an impartial enquiry into the harassment of Christians of Arunachal during the last ten years.

We again earnestly request you to maintain the secular image of the nation and we the Arunachal Pradesh Christians should also be protected and safeguarded as guaranteed under the Constitution.

Sd/- Wanglat Lowangcha
Chairman
Arunachal Christian Action Committee

Sd/- L. M. Yanger
Secretary
Arunachal Christian Action Committee

Sd/- Mading Laling
Treasurer
Arunachal Christian Action Committee

Sd/- Y. Lego
Member—A. C. A. C.

Sd/- Tadar Taniang
Member—A. C. A. C.

Sd/- Aggong Ratan
Member—A. C. A. C.

Sd/- T. Ering
Member—A. C. A. C.

Document 28:

To,
   The Leader of the Study Team, Members of Parliament
   Arunachal Pradesh

Dated: Itanagar/Ziro the 10th of April, 1979

Sub:- Memorandum submitted to the Members of Parliament in the matter of the religious Freedom in Arunachal Pradesh.

Hon'ble Members of Parliament,
I on behalf of the Christian Community of Subansiri District would like to draw your special kind attention to the following lines for your sympathetic consideration and action as the study team.

   Christianity entered and Church growth started in 1960 in Subansiri District and the first Church was established in Tale village in 1963, even though there were converts before that period. It is recorded the first convert was Shri Tabia Begi, in 1926 and followed by other 12 persons.

   After the Independence, 1947, there were many other converts and number of Christians started growing. In the fifties many students were converted at North Lakhimpur Mission School, who led the Christians of Subansiri District as Church leaders.

Now there are about 5,000 baptized Church members and many new converts. Therefore, age of Christianity in Subansiri District is more than life age of our Independence.

Since entry of Christianity began, it has been a tradition for the administrative officials to be involved in encouraging the non-Christian local leaders to oppose the entry of Christianity in the District. The best example can be had in the persons of Mr. Harban Singh and Jagir Singh. Harban Singh, a Home Guard Officer who encouraged the local Home Guard personal to set fire in Churches in January 1969 in Ziro area. Another Government officer named Jagir (E. A. C.) of Sagalee, who had been involved in anti-religious activities in Sagalee area is true witness. He had not only instigated the non-Christian local people but also seized the Bibles from Christian people and had severely beaten Teche Epe just because he had accepted the Christian faith, who refused to give it up, in 25.1.1971.

In 1972, Shri Idkha Takha of Pania village in Ziro area was arrested by the Panchayat members of Subansiri district on 3.5.1972 and on 8.5.1972 another five Christian people were taken as prisoners. Christian representatives approached the Deputy Commissioner of Subansiri, Mr. T. C. Hazarika, he did not assure any sort of protection rather gathered a good number of people who deadly opposed the Christian faith and no justice was done to Christian people in perfect sense of safeguard. Shri Tadar Tang, Vice-President of Subansiri took away the second group of Christian: 1. Debia Chetum, 2. Debia Takha, 3. Toko Dedum, 4. Khoda Takha, to Palin area and kept them there for 80 days. They had received a worse treatment from persecutors and many times they were asked to work without food. D. C. could have saved them easily.

In 1975, 11th December, the D. C. of Subansiri issued an order banning the construction of churches and the copy of the same enclosed herewith. D. C. came to Cher village on 1st of February 1976 and personally declared that no Church gathering or construction of any Church. He also told that Christianity was a foreign religion and cannot be practiced by Indian people since it was a foreign religion, not Indian. He also told the Nishi people should better accept Buddhism than Christianity. He even went to state that Christian people are trouble-maker. The Christian people of Cher village submitted a petition seeking permission for construction of a Church in their village and later on DC posted a written reply to the petitioners in 28.2.1976. (Copy enclosed).

In 29.9.1977, Lt. Governor of Arunachal Pradesh came to Cher to inaugurate the Vivekananda School and told Shri Ter Tana of Cher village not to preach his religion, if he did so, he was warned for that cause. He said, "Be careful, be careful, be careful," to Shri Ter Tana for nothing. Then Ter Tana said whether the Lt. Governor could give any reason why he should be careful. But the Lt. Governor could say no reason and departed ahead.

During 1974 persecution, government servants who accepted Christian faith were left unprotected. Their dwelling houses were burned down and many of them received harassment, for example; Shri Khoda Tana of Doimukh, Shri Ter Tana, Shri Duli Tana of Cher, were left unprotected. The Panchayat members too suffered severe persecutions who were Christians. Shri Khoda Tana an employee of Arunachal Pradesh Secretariat, Itanagar, was dragged out of the Circle Officer's Office of Doimukh who did not do anything for him.

In 1974 persecution, the extra Assistant Commissioner, Sagalee, the Deputy Commissioner, Ziro, the Circle Officer of Doimukh and Circle Officer, Kimin and many other Government officers did not do any function of real justice rather remained anti-religious agents and encouraged the persecutors directly or indirectly.

In 5.9.78, Shri Likha Takha was caught by Shri Benggia Telum and others on the following day he was taken to Chulyue village on 7.9.1979. The persecutors took hold of all Christian people of that village and tied them to posts in the burning sunlight for the whole day and Christian people were forced to renounce their faith in the spot without any cause. Incident has been reported to the Deputy Commissioner of Ziro by the Subansiri Baptist Christian Convention, Secretary on 19th Sept. '78 but no action has been so far reported, in the line concerned.

Therefore when Panchayat members are asked that why they interfere and persecute the Christian people they say it was an order from D. C. and Mr. Tadar Tang, D. C. and Mr. Tadar Tang had asked them to oppose the Christian faith and therefore they did it on behalf of them. Persons who say this story are the following out of many: 1. Shri Tikha Serbi, A. S. M. of Site village, 2. Shri Likha Pen, G. B. of Miya village, 3. Shri Likha of Kugitaga, 4. Shri Tagi Tayer, Tage village, 5. Shri Tana Epe, A. S. M. of Teru.

Therefore, in the past administrative officials were very much involved in the anti-religious activities no doubt; but now the passing of the Arunachal Freedom of Indigenous Religion Act, 1978, has given the officers more power and opportunities to act at a fast rate against the Christians of Arunachal Pradesh. The administrative officers were and are the root cause of all misunderstanding and nefarious activities between the Christians and non-Christians. Therefore, administrative officers must declare publicly the Freedom of Right to Religion enshrined in the Constitution of our country.

The Arunachal Pradesh Freedom of Religion Act, 1978 should be repealed if the Government of Arunachal Pradesh deems to provide peaceful co-existence of all sections of religious community in harmony and unity that accelerate the degree of development in years to come.

The existing Christian people should be given permission to gather and their worship services in their village Churches and volunteer conversion should be allowed who seek for it. And the persons who created misunderstandings between the Christians and the non-Christians should be punished and called for his or deed.

Some lists of properties that were destroyed during 1974 persecution are enclosed herewith for your information and knowledge and for necessary action on the lines stated above.

On behalf of the Christians of Subansiri District.

(Shri Ter Tana Tara)
Executive Secretary,
Subansiri Baptist Convention, Subansiri District.

Dated: Lakhimpur the 10th April, 1979

Document 29:

Dated Ziro, the 12th April, 1979

To
   The Deputy Commissioner Khonsa, Tirap District, Arunachal

Subject: Persecution on Christian in Tirap District, Arunachal

Sir,
We the undersigned have the honour to inform you that the following incident happened in Mopaghat village during March 26th 1979.

The anti-Christians demolished one Church building at Mopaghat. Also Mr. Lenguih house cut and left potentials laying ruin. His wife also pull out from her house while her husband out. He was transferred recently to an afar distance to Kameng District.

The Church was erected in December 11, 1977, which is an old Church and they dismantled all the Church property which is rendered useless.

The following individual property dismantled.

> One cane chair
> One house (chicken farm)
> Two ploughing Cows
> One pig cost Rs.300/-

The following were the leaders:

> Kanubari C. O.
> Agriculture Officer Kanubari
> Political Jamatar Kanubari
> Kotoki Kanubari
> Benbhara Roja & Gaon Bora.

We therefore, the Wancho Baptist Church Council earnestly request the honourable Deputy Commissioner Khonsa to give proper correction to the encroacher and give safety to this minority Christian in the area.

Yours faithfully
WBCC Members

Copy to:

D. C. Khonsa
A. P. O. Kanubari
C. O. Kanubari
CBCNEI General Secretary
NBCC Executive Secretary
ABAM Executive Secretary
TBCC Executive Secretary
MLA Nokchong Poham
MLA Wangnam Wangsho

1. I. Toshi Pastor Barigaon
2. Podmo Deobani
3. Aram Mopaghat
4. Mr. Mankai Zotsa
5. Sanlim Barigaon
6. Rev. I. Longsa

Document 30:

ARUNACHAL CHRISTIAN ACTION COMMITTEE
ARUNACHAL PRADESH

Dated the April 17th 1979
Camp Dibrugarh

This Committee pledged to function as a link between the various groups of Christians in the State of Arunachal Pradesh. Its duty shall be to protect the rights of the minorities Christians of Arunachal. To oppose the Arunachal Freedom of Religion Bill Act 1978 which has been legalized to persecute and discriminate the Arunachal Christians. This Committee demands the protection of Arunachal Christians as granted by the Indian Constitution. It is also resolved that the Arunachal cultural heritage can be preserved even with the growth of Christianity.

Office bearers of the Executive Committee
Chairman: Mr. J. W. Lowangcha

Secretary: Mr. L. M. Yanger
Treasurer: Mr. Madang Latin

Executive Members:
Mr. Yonthem Lego
Mr. Aggong Ratan
Mr. Tapon Ering
Mr. Tadar Taniang
Mr. Khoda Tana
Mr. Neelam Taran

Resolutions

A legal advisor be sought who could go to Arunachal Pradesh to find facts.

The local leader of each Committee (district) shall assist the legal advisor when he visits the respective areas. The local leaders are :

Mr. T. M. Laling and Mr. R. T. Tanaing for Subansiri Dist.
Mr. Aggong Rattan for Siang Dist.
Mr. Yonthem Lego for Lohit Dist.
Mr. L. M. Yanger for Tirap Dist.

There should be publicity to cover the following :
Explanation of the meaning of Christianity
Appeal for help
Person in charge of Publicity: The secretary of ACAC. The Publicity should be translated into regional language by the ACAC members.

To explore the feasibility of instituting a legal case against the memorandum submitted by Tekar Techi. Tadar Tanya will consult a lawyer for taking a suitable action. Shri Khoda Tana may be appellant.

Finance: To be raise funds from contribution—individual well wishers.

Appeals be made to all church and individuals with minimum one rupee from each person within Arunachal.

Appeals be made to all interdenominational Church bodies for help.

The decision of ACAC be included in the appeals to the Joint Action Committee of the NEI.

To open a Bank Account in Dibrugarh SBI with immediate effect.

There should be two signatures. The Chairman and the Secretary have been given the authority to sign on behalf of the ACAC for withdrawal cheques only.

The treasurer should keep all the Accounts and Secretary should intimate all the financial transactions to Treasurer immediately.

The Executive Members are entitled for travelling allowance depending on financial position.

The present temporary office shall be located at Bishop's House, Dibrugarh with a typist-cum steno.

Students Cell

Each local Church leader will have to mobilize the students and make good contacts.

Counter student Union be organized against anti-Christian Student Organization.

Educate the people through meetings and seminars.

The next venue for ACAC meeting has been fixed in Shillong in consultation with the joint Action Committee of NEI.

Selected Members:

1. Wanglat Lowangcha	14. J. P. Jugli
2. Tadar Taniang	15. Nongtu Lungphi
3. M. Lalin	16. Rangkom Ronrang
4. Yonthem Lego	17. Baimn Mungrang
5. L. M. Yanger	18. Molem Ronrang
6. Aggong Ratan	19. Makai Wancho
7. Tapon Ering	20. Khoda Tana
8. Gengken Riba	21. Neelam Taram
9. Mito Riba	22. Toso Grayo
10. Dojing Pangam	23. Kas Tako
11. P. Lowang	24. Tagey Tokom
12. Kuku Lego	25. Aran Wancho
13. Tero Kakho	

The above resolutions were passed and accepted.

Wanglat Lowangcha, Chairman
L. M. Yanger, Secretary
Mudang Laling, Treasurer
Yonthem Lego, Member
Aggong Ratan, - do-
Tapon Ering, - do-
Tadar Tanyang, - do-

Document 31:

AN APPEAL TO ALL CHRISTIANS IN INDIA AND ELSEWHERE FROM THE CHURCH LEADERS OF ARUNACHAL PRADESH

Dear Friends,

On 16th April, 1979 Christian Leaders from Arunachal Pradesh held a meeting at Bishop's House, Dibrugarh in the presence of important Christian MPs and Church leaders. This meeting resolved the urgent necessity of forming a nucleus within the State of Arunachal Pradesh and a Committee was formed in the name and style Arunachal Christian Action Committee with a Chairman, a Secretary, a Treasurer and 6 executive members. This Committee was formed because of the untold story of persecutions that has been going on and is still of the Christian communities of Arunachal Pradesh.

Some of the few glaring instances of persecutions in Arunachal Pradesh are:

1. The process of persecutions are not only of recent events but it has been enforced since 1969, e.g. on 7.01.69 Deed, Nelam and Saya Churches in Ziro area were burnt by the members of the home-guard on the order of Shri Harbans Singh, a home-guard commander. It was reported to D.C. of Ziro but he refused to take any action.
2. On 23.01.79, Shri Jagir Singh, the present EAC (Sr.), Roing ordered Lowant Wang, V. L. W. to assault Talo Sakha of Tarso village for no reason except that he is a Christian.

3. On 6.02.72, Shri Tasar Mangha assaulted Byabian Ringeho because he was a Christian. On the same day Shri Mangha stripped naked Smt. Leggbia Yapu in public for refusing to renounce Christianity. The matter was brought before the D. C. but the D. C. refused to take notice and dismissed the matter without taking any action.
4. On 19.03.74, Naharlagun Church was burnt on the order of Tadar Tang, the present Supply and Transport Minister, Arunachal Pradesh. His accomplices are Shri Tachi Takang, Zilla Parishad Member, Thana Epo and Techi Dodum. It may be noted that Naharlagun is at the outskirt of Itanagar, the new capital of Arunachal Pradesh.
5. On 21st July 1978, Shri Aram Wancho, a Christian of Mopaghat area had to suffer injustice in the hands of the persecutors. His son's dead body was not allowed to be buried or to perform the last rites as a Christian in the territory of Arunachal Pradesh. As a result of this the mourning father had to carry his son's dead body from his home land to the state of Assam so that his son may rest in peace.
6. On 21st February 1979, three persons were arrested under the Section 3 of Arunachal Religion Act 1978. They are Hapjong Jugli, Tukhim Jugli and Hangkam Jugli. They were confined under the C. R. P. lock up for 30 days. They were released after forcing them to put their thumb impression on a petition which alleged that they have renounced their faith. Their Church was pulled down when they were under C. R. P. custody.
7. On 26th March 1979, one Church was burnt in Mopaghat of Tirap District. Along with this a pig belonging to a Christian family was forcefully killed and two ploughing

bulls were taken away and various household articles were destroyed.

To fight out these injustices we request all the Christians in India and elsewhere and also to all right thinking people for the country to:

Pray earnestly and unitedly for the People of Arunachal Pradesh so that their faith in Christ may be firmed like a rock and also for the success of the movement against the Anti Conversion Laws in all parts of India;

To enable us to work for those who are suffering we urge you to contribute liberally.

Arunachal Christian Action Committee

Contributions may please be sent to:

The ACAC,
C/O Fr. Joseph V. M.
Bishop's House
Dibrugarh—786 001

Document 32:

NORTH-EAST INDIA ACTION COMMITTEE
FOR RELIGIOUS FREEDOM

C/O NEICC Office, Dinam Hall, Jaiaw, Shillong—793002
Or Archbishop's House, Shillong—793003

April 19, 1979

An Assembly of Church Leaders of North-East India gathered at the Archbishop's House on April 5, 1979, decided to call for a Hartal to be observed all over North-East India, in protest against the Freedom of Religion Bill introduced in the Parliament by Shri O. P. Tyagi and the harassment of Christians in Arunachal Pradesh.

Our reasons for the objection to the Freedom of Religion Bill are many (please see the handbill "A Bill has been introduced in the Parliament").

Though Shri H. M. Patel said on the floor of the Parliament that there has been no harassment of Christians in Arunachal Pradesh, we have too many evidences to show that the contrary is the truth. Added to that, we are deeply disappointed that the Prime Minister, while in Shillong recently (April 7), rejected the plea of Church leaders for the institution of an enquiry into the allegations of harassment of Christians in Arunachal Pradesh.

Recently (April 10–16) four Christian MP's (Mrs. Rano Shaiza, Mr. G. S. Reddy, Mr. P. A. Sangma, Mr. H. Lyngdoh) visited Arunachal Pradesh and saw for themselves the plight of the Christians in the Union Territory. They had opportunity to interview a large number of people who have been victims of persecution.

All these add new meaning to our call for a hartal which will be peaceful. Clear instructions are being given to the team of volunteers that they ensure the Hartal goes off without any untoward incident.

The Hartal should start from the minute it strikes 12 midnight (ushering the 3rd of May) and should go on till 3:00 pm. At 4:00 pm a rally must be held at all strategic centres.

We have appealed to all believers in secularism to lend us their support. We have invited men of every faith and political point of view to join us.

We have already the support of various tribal youth associations: Meghalaya Tribal Youth Organization, Mizo, Garo, Bodo, Naga and other youth federations. The CPI has come forward promising their support. We are writing to Vice-Chancellors of all universities of North-East India explaining the reason of the hartal and asking for their co-operation.

We have already news that similar efforts are being made at Tura, Jowai, Kohima, Dimapur, Imphal, Aizawl and other places.

The cause we are fighting for is not a Christian cause. It is a cause dear to everyone who loves the unity of India. Take away the spirit of secularism enshrined in the Constitution and you have sown the seeds of disruption all over the land. Would it be wise to sow such dangerous seeds all along the Border States?

Rev. Fr. Thomas Menamparampil &
P. B. M. Basaiawmoit
Secretary of
NEIAC, Shillong

Document 33:

MEMORANDUM SUBMITTED BY THE CHRISTIAN CO-ORDINATING COMMITTEE, DIBRUGARH, TO THE DEPUTY COMMISSIONER OF DIBRUGARH

Respected Sir,

We the Christian Co-coordinating Committee of Dibrugarh, representing the various Christian Denominations of Dibrugarh and Sibsagar Districts in Assam and of Tirap and Lohit Sub-Divisions in Arunachal Pradesh as well as Christians throughout India, united as a single body, wish to draw your attention to the following:

We strongly protest against the treatment being meted out to our fellow Christians in Arunachal Pradesh. They are being subjected to constant harassment on account of their religious belief. The Christians of Arunachal Pradesh are prevented from holding religious services, from constructing places of worship and from performing other legitimate religious acts.

We further consider all restrictions of the freedom of religion as unconstitutional, undemocratic and unworthy of a great country like ours.

The Freedom of Religion Act '78 of Arunachal Pradesh has furnished a powerful weapon to the forces hostile to Christians to indulge in anti-Christian activities under cover of the said Act.

The Administrative machinery has frequently been used to force Christians to give up their religion. Such actions are gross violations of the right of the citizens and an abuse of authority. All this is becoming more and more evident as the days pass.

> Article 25 of the Indian Constitution affirms that "all persons are equally entitled to freedom of conscience and the right to freely profess, practice and propagate religion."
>
> Article 26 states "every religious denomination or any section thereof shall have the right— (b)—to manage its own affairs in matters of religion."
>
> Article 18 of the Universal Declaration of Human Rights says: "Everyone has the right to freedom of thought, conscience and religion; this right includes freedom to change his religion or belief."

But the "Arunachal Pradesh Freedom of Religion Act" and "Freedom of Religion" now pending before the Parliament to prevent the free exercise of the rights guaranteed to all religions under Article 25 of the Indian constitution and under Article 18 of the Declaration of Human Rights as mentioned above. The so called "Freedom of Religion Bill" in question are not intended at all to prevent conversions by force, fraud or inducement as they pretend, but in reality are intended in their operation, to prevent any conversion at all by introducing a reign of Police Raj in the sphere of religion.

Why should the Government interfere in the choice and practice of religion of a citizen? Why should a citizen report his choice of religion to any Government officer? Why should a citizen be hindered from being a Christian or embrace any other religion? Why should there be raised a hue and cry against the Christians and the Christian Missionaries without any justification as if they act otherwise than in accordance with the principle of their own Religion, which believes in and profess the principles of Freedom, Justice and Love.

We therefore make the following demand:

> That the iniquitous Freedom of Religion Act in Arunachal Pradesh be immediately repealed.
>
> That the proposed Freedom of Religion Bill in the Parliament be totally withdrawn.
>
> That an impartial Parliamentary Commission including Christian members of the Lok Sabha and Rajya Sabha be set up immediately to investigate the injustices being inflicted on the Christians in Arunachal Pradesh, which is more than evident, so that justice and freedom may be restored to them without delay.

We therefore, request you as representative of the Government to forward this petition to the President of India, to the Governor of Arunachal Pradesh and to the Governor of Assam.

Sd/- Shri S. Ignatius Ekka
Chairman
Christian Co-ordinating Committee, Dibrugarh

Document 34:

PRESS RELEASE

24th April, 1979

The Working Committee of the Catholic Union of India met at Bangalore on the 21st and 22nd instant under the leadership of the National President, Mr. D. V. D'Monte, MLC. Present for the meeting were Mr. G. S. Reddy, M. P., Dr. A. Sequire, Vice President, Bombay, Mr. L. Stuart, Vice-President, Calcutta, Captain Mathias, National Secy., Mr. Jayachandraraj, Executive Secy., Mr. Joseph, Vice-President, Kerala, Mr. Coutinho, Vice-President, Karnataka. The Catholic Union received a report from Mr. G. S. Reddy on the atrocities committed against Christians in Arunachal Pradesh, Bihar also in regard to the burning of Churches, the murder of a priest and a persecution of lay-leaders.

The Catholic Union reconsidered the Freedom of Religion Bill of Mr. O. P. Tyagi, M. P., and has chalked out an action bound programme for the withdrawal of this Bill.

The important features of the programme are as follows:

To have a high power meeting of Christians, Muslims, Buddhists, Members of Parliament in Delhi during the first week of May.

To undertake a morcha before parliament comprising of Christian leaders, Members of Parliament and others.

All Catholic Union State units throughout the country to undertake Satyagraha and fasting on a date to be notified

Sd/-

National President
Catholic Union of India

Document 35:

BISHOP'S HOUSE
DIBRUGARH, ASSAM, INDIA
12th June '79

To
    The Deputy Commissioner
    Khonsa
    Tirap Dist.
    ARUNACHAL PRADESH.

SUBJECT: PETITION FOR INNER LINE PERMIT

Dear Sir,
I am a Christian Priest and would like to minister the Christians living in Tirap Dist.

Therefore I request you to issue me an inner line permit as per rules.

The necessary particulars are given below:

Name	: Fr. Job
Surname	: Kallarackal
Father's name	: K. J. Thomas
Age	: 30 years
Nationality	: Indian
Permanent Address	: Bishop's House

Dibrugarh, Assam

Thanking you,

Yours faithfully,

Fr. Job Kallarackal

* The application was rejected, which made him enter Nokfan Village taking the Borhat jungle track and to travel some distance by boat along the Tissa River. Subsequently, he was arrested and convicted.

Document 36:

PROCEEDINGS OF THE GENERAL ASSEMBLY OF THE CHRISTIAN LEADERS, NORTH-EAST INDIA PRESBYTERIAN CHURCH, POLICE BAZAAR, SHILLONG

JUNE 29, 1979

I. The meeting was presided over by Rt. Rev. D. D. Pradhan, C. N. I., Bishop of Assam diocese.

II. PRESIDENTIAL SPEECH

At the very outset, the President accorded warm welcome to all in particular to Messrs. Hoping Stone Lyngdoh (MP of Shillong) and Bakin Pertin (MP from Arunachal), to Revds. K. I. Aier & D. Bhuyan, who are attending for the first time.

In the course of his speech, Bishop Pradhan expressed his congratulation and satisfaction in the uniformed struggle, the Church in India had shown during the last few months. He added that the government of India is awed at the spontaneity, unity, alertness and ability of the Christians to mobilize public opinion against the Religion Bill, not only in India but in overseas too.

He however stressed that our struggle is not over; rather we need to march ahead and consider more steps of action. He cautioned the assembly that there should be no room for complacency. Hence this Assembly, he pointed out that this Assembly has been called in order to formulate strategies of action further strengthen the cause.

III. DEVOTION

Rev. Fr. Sngi Lyngdoh led in the devotions, stressing the fact that Jesus Christ's prayer that all his followers may be one as He and the Father are one, should be made an attempt to be made by this assembly in that oneness in spirit must be seen in all of us, despite the varieties of backgrounds and traditions.

IV. INTRODUCTORY WORDS

His grace, the Archbishop of Shillong-Gauhati Archdiocese, Dr. Hubert D'Rozario, delivered the introductory speech. In the course of his address, he informed the Assembly that the Church in Europe is very much concerned over the developments in India, particularly, over the Government's attempt to curtail Religious Freedom. At the same time, the Pope in Rome, is very happy to learn that in this struggle for Religious Freedom, the Christians in India are being drawn closer to one another, and encourage the fight for man's fundamental right must continue at all cost. Archbishop D'Rozario further informed that the Pope admonished that we need to turn more to God. He further observed that in fact, through this attempt to curtail religious freedom, many more men and women are coming to know the Gospel of Jesus Christ.

The Archbishop reminded that once we were strangers but now we have become friends and have come to know each other quite well.

V. REPORT FROM THE SECRETARIES

Mr. P. B. M. Basaiawmoit, one of the Secretaries, gave the report on the work carried out since April, 1979. He informed the Assembly that the Action Committee had appointed three other committees, viz. the Law Cell, Publicity Committee and Finance Committee. However the function of the Finance Committee has been hampered with the resignation of the Treasurer. Otherwise the other Committees have been carrying their responsibilities exceptionally well.

Further, an open letter to Messrs. O. P. Tyagi (author of the Bill) and H. M. Patel (Union Home Minister) had been sent by the Secretary. He added that letters were sent to the Chief Ministers of Meghalaya, Manipur, Mizoram & Nagaland, requesting them to lend support in protesting against Tyagi's Bill and till now, the Manipur and Nagaland's Cabinet have passed resolutions to the effect and the Meghalaya Assembly had passed a similar resolution on June 28 '79. Meanwhile, Mizoram is still to do so.

The Secretary further informed the Assembly that according to reports received, the demonstrations arranged during May 1979, in the whole of N. E. India have been very successful. In addition many letters of encouragement and enquiry have been received by the Secretaries.

VI. REPORT OF THE PUBLICITY COMMITTEE

Fr. Thomas Menamparampil, the other Secretary gave the report of the Publicity Committee. He informed that a large number of pamphlets and booklets pertaining to atrocities meted out to Christians in Arunachal Pradesh, facts about Christianity and pamphlets pertaining to curtailment of religious freedom have been published and distributed widely in the region, in India and overseas.

Further as the committee was given the charge of the Hartal, processions and various types of demonstrations in N. E. India, therefore, was kept busy in its working.

VII. REPORT OF THE FINANCE COMMITTEE

Mr. P. B. M. Basaiawmoit reported that the Finance Committee was slightly hampered in its working with resignation of the Treasurer and up till now a Treasurer has not been found.

However the work of the Finance Committee has been carried out by the two Secretaries.

He reported that a Bank Account has been opened in the name of NEIJACRF at the Vijaya Bank, Shillong. He further informed the Assembly that financial support has been encouraging, particularly from Manipur and North Cachar Hills.

VIII. REPORT FROM THE LAW CELL

Mr. M. S. Jahrin (Advocate), convener of the Law Cell informed the Assembly that it is necessary for the law cell to receive all the documents that can serve as incriminating evidences for study before deciding on registering a case in any court. He added that somebody who is directly affected should file a case otherwise there will not be any locus standi.

He suggested that there should be a legal advisor stationed somewhere in Tezpur, near Arunachal Pradesh and that someone should be appointed to collect all the available facts and documents. In addition for a start, a defamation case should be registered in the high Court against Takar Techi for his allegations and undermining the credibility of Christianity.

IX. REPORT FROM THE ARUNACHAL CHRISTIAN ACTION COMMITTEE
(SEE APPENDIX 'B')

X. FUTURE OF O. P. TYAGI'S BILL

Mr. H. S. Lyngdoh, MP, highlighted on the future standing of Om Prakash Tyagi's Religion Bill.

Mr. Lyngdoh informed the Assembly that if at all the Bill is to be discussed, since it is a Private Member's Bill, knowledge of it being taken up will be known one week in advance. As it is, unless the Bill is withdrawn, it will remain in the custody of the

House till the present Parliament is dissolved. As such it will not be proper to keep quiet. Further, if the Government is bent on introducing a "better Bill" it will be more serious and therefore our struggle should be intensified and this Assembly should come to some decision on action to be followed.

As it is now, the Janata Party is a divided house, but we should not rest assured on this state of affairs of the building of the Ruling Party. The Government too is really alarmed at the hue and cry raised all over India in opposition of the Religion Bill, but the voice of the people should continue to knock at the doors of Parliament so that the Government will have a second thought on legislating a Bill.

As Freedom of Religion is a national issue, all Christian MLAs and MPs should be kept informed on all events of harassment, persecution in the name of the religion anywhere in India, and further, these legislators should be taken into confidence.

XI. HELP TO OUR ARUNACHAL BRETHREN

Mr. L. M. Yanger, Secretary ACAC, proposed the following:

- Legal litigation should take place very soon
- A management and leadership seminar should be held in Arunachal for Christian Youth and Church Leaders.
- A youth cell as suggested in the report should be created with the help of the NEI Jt. Action Committee
- There should be exchange visits to Arunachal Pradesh as this will help getting to know one another and would develop brotherhood and national integrity.

XII. RESOLUTIONS
A. FINANCE: RESOLVED:

- That Mr. Friday Lyngdoh be appointed Treasurer in place of Rev C. Jyrwa who has resigned.

- That the delegates coming from Arunachal be granted travelling expense of Rs. 1,500/- (Rupees One Thousand Five Hundred) only lump sum.
- That initially, Rs.5,000 (Rupees Five Thousand) only be budgeted for the Law Cell.

B. LEGAL: RESOLVED:

- That Mr. Tadar Taniang be appointed to travel around Arunachal to collect facts and documents pertaining to atrocities meted out to Christians in Arunachal Pradesh.
- That the Law Cell completes all its studies and preparations for filing cases within one month.
- That a defamation case be filed in the High Court against Takar Techi for his wrongful and malicious allegations of Christianity in his memorandum to the President of India.
- That all possible legal aid be given to Arunachal Christian Action Committee for its legal battle against the various orders given by the Arunachal Government intimidating Christians in that Union Territory.

C. OTHER ACTIONS: RESOLVED:

- That in O. P. Tyagi's Bill still pending in Parliament and that there is every likelihood of the Central Government including its own Religion Bill, the Christian Community in India, in general, and in N. E. India, in particular, be alert and ready to take up the following lines of action:
- During the week in which the Bill may be discussed in Parliament, united prayer meetings be held in every part of N. E. India, for about four consecutive evenings.

- For three days, Christian schools, colleges and technical Institutions remain closed as a mark of protest.
- Wherever possible, and if necessary, Christian/Church leaders stage dharna in front of Governor's residences/ Civil Secretariats/Collectorates/Dy. Commissioners'/S. D. O.s' offices.
- A day before the Bill is to be discussed in the Parliament, mammoth rallies are held all over N. E. India at State Capitals/Districts/Sub-Divisional Headquarters.
- Christian Members of Parliament are requested immediately to convey news of the proposed Bill being taken up in Parliament to the Christian leaders of their respective States/Constituencies, NCCI, CBCI Action Committee, Regional& Local Action Committees for immediate preparation and uniformed action.
- That the Chief Ministers of Manipur, Meghalaya, Nagaland and Mizoram be contacted for their unstinted support and for a possibility of having a meeting of all Christian MPs in India and Christian MLAs in N. E. India, at a place to be chalked out with them for united effort to protect and safeguard and fundamental rights and secular image of India.

XIII. VOTE OF THANKS:
Rev. K. I. Aier proposed the vote of thanks particularly expressing appreciation for Fr. Thomas Menamparampil's whole hearted effort in carrying out the work of the Action Committee mainly through the Publicity Committee. He also thanked the two Members of Parliament for sparing their time and contributing so much to the Assembly through their experience and

also the Khasi Jaintia Presbyterian Synod for allowing the use of their Church Building for this Assembly. He also expressed thanks to all who have come and made this Assembly a success, and above all to God, who made it possible for this meeting to be held.

XIV. CLOSING:
Archbishop Hubert D'Rozario offered the closing prayer and benediction.

Shillong: July 5, 1979.

P. B. M. Basaiawmoit

■ ■ ■

REPORT FROM THE ARUNACHAL CHRISTION ACTION COMMITTEE

This Committee pledged to function as a link between the various groups of Christians in the state of Arunachal Pradesh. Its duty shall be to protect the rights of the minority Christians of Arunachal. To oppose the Arunachal Freedom of Religion Bill 1978 which has been legalized to persecute and discriminate the Arunachal Christians. This Committee demands the protection of Arunachal Christians as granted by the Indian Constitution. It is also resolved that Arunachal cultural heritage can be preserved even with the growth of Christianity.

OFFICE BEARERS OF THE EXECUTIVE COMMITTEE
Chairman:- Mr. J. W. Lowangcha
Secretary:- Mr. L. M. Yanger
Treasurer:- Mr. T. M. Taling

EXECUTIVE MEMBERS
1. Mr. Yonthem Lego, 2. Mr. Angong Ratan, 3. Mr. Tapon Ering, 4. Mr. R. T. Taniang, 5. Mr. Khoda Tana, 6. Mr. Talam Neelam

RESOLUTIONS :
A legal advisor be sought who would go to Arunachal Pradesh to find out facts.

The local leader of each Committee (District) shall be the with the legal advisor [CE24] when he visits the respective areas. The local leaders are: -

i. Messrs. T. M. Laling and R. T. Taniang for Subansiri Dist.
ii. Mr. Angong Ratan for Siang
iii. Mr. Yongthem Lego for Lohit
iv. Mr. L. M. Yanger for Tirap

There should be publicity to cover the following :

Explanation of the term of Christianity
Appeal for help
Person in charge of publicity: The Secretary

Publicity should be translated into regional language by the ACAC members.

To explore the feasibility of instituting a legal case against the memorandum submitted by Takar Techi. Tadar Tanyang will consult a lawyer for taking a suitable action. Shri Khoda Tana may be appellant.

FINANCE :
To raise funds

Appeals be made to all committees and individuals with minimum one rupee from each person within Arunachal

Appeals be made to all interdenominational Church bodies for help

The decision of the ACAC be included in the appeals to the Joint Action Committee of NEI

To open a Bank Account in Dibrugarh SBI with immediate effect.

The present temporary office shall be located at Bishop House, Dibrugarh with a typist cum steno.

Students Cell

Each local Church leader will have to mobilize the students and make good contacts

Select student leaders for visiting important historical places

Counter Student Union be organized against anti-Christian Student Organization.

Sd/- L. M. Yanger
Secretary ACAC

Document 37:

LIEUTENANT GOVERNOR—ARUNACHAL PRADESH
RAJ NIWAS
ITANAGAR—791 111

D.O. NO. LG/PS-P/79
JULY 15TH 1979

My Dear Rano,

By now you might have received my letter dated the 3rd May '79. I was hoping to write to you once again but frequent tours in the interior and other preoccupations kept me rather busy.

I got the complaint you have forwarded under your letter of 27th April. We enquired into the matter and the reports from the concerned district authorities have since been received. Although you did not request for any reports, I thought it would be desirable to let you know the position. The gist of the report can be seen at Annexure A, B and C.

I had also an occasion to visit Miao, Nampong, Manmao and Changlang in Tirap district. I met a large number of local people at all these places. Except at Miao nowhere had the local people mentioned about religion. Even in Miao when one of the local people complained of hindrance, I had asked the people present to give specific instances of interference of their religious practices. None, however, cited any instance. The person who mentioned about it hails from Songking village where there is already a Church. The Field Secretary of Tirap Baptist Church Council, Shri L. M. Yanger has also been freely moving around not only in these areas but also in other parts of Arunachal Pradesh.

Since my arrival I have been vigilant about the fairness and just claims of people of different predilections. I cannot vouchsafe that in a vast territory like ours we shall be able to able to establish the "Kingdom of God" or *"Ramrajya"* —a perfectly integrated and peaceful society. There will always be some incidents which may be caused by either local feuds or clashes of culture or of personality. There are however elements in society who might communalize and magnify their vested interest. I am sure, with your vast experience as a social worker and now as an MP, who has gone around and seen various parts of the country, you will see this matter in totality and appreciate the need to a fragmentary approach to this problem. I from my side already impressed on all concerned, particularly our district and local officers, the need to be fair and just and not serve any sectional interests.

I would like to request you once again to direct those who come and complained to you about maltreatment, harassment or interference to meet me and place their problems squarely before me without any mental reservations. I can assure you that any genuine complaint would be promptly looked into and necessary action taken.

I also reiterate that the vast majority of the people of AP are greatly concerned about preservation and promotion of their traditional culture and faith. I had mentioned this in my earlier letter to you. We must respect their sentiments. No one should be encouraged to belittle or look down upon their age old cultural heritage and thus provoke them to react. If there is basic understanding, I am sure even the stray incidents which sometimes erupt could be eliminated.

Incidentally, your sister Leno (Mrs. Terhuja) had written a thesis entitled "Faith? Reason and Culture." Will you kindly request her to spare me a copy for my perusal?

Itanagar
16 July '79

* The above letter was written by R. N. Haldipur to Ms. Rano Saiza, MP, Nagaland.

Document 38:

CRASH W.T.

TO
  THE DC, KSA
  FR. EAC, LDG
  NO.CA/13

AS PER YOUR INSTRUCTION ONE CHURCH AT NIAUSA VILLAGE DISMANTLED COMPLETELY THROUGH VILLAGERS (.) ALLEDGED AFFORDS ARRESTED BY POLICE RELEASED ON P.R. BOND (.)

HAGE KHODA, EAC
1ST CLASS MAGISTRATE
LDG

Document 39:

To,
  The DC
  Khonsa, Tirap Dist.
  Arunachal Pradesh.

Sub: Inner Line Permit.

Sir,
On 2nd Aug '79 we would like to perform the "HUM WANG" ceremony of our chapel (Catholic) at Borduria village. Therefore

we want the Rt. Rev. Bishop of Dibrugarh and other Rev. Fathers to come and bless the Chapel on the occasion. As such I on behalf of the Tirap Catholic Church Association request you to kindly issue Inner Line Permit Pass to the following persons. Please note that all the names given are Indian Nationals. I/L Pass may be kindly issued for a week i.e. 31st July—6th Aug '79.

Rev. Bishop Kerketta, Bishop House, Dibrugarh, Assam
Rev. Bishop J. Mittathany, Bishop's House, Tezpur, Assam
Rev. Fr. T. Menamparampil, Director Don Bosco Tech. School, C/o Bishop House, Dibrugarh, Assam
Rev. Fr. J. Kallarachal, Bishop House, Dibrugarh, Assam
Rev. Fr. George, Don Bosco School, Naharkatiya, Assam
Rev. Fr. Joseph, Bishop House, Dibrugarh, Assam
Rev. Fr. Mathew, Provincial House, Don Bosco School, Gauhati, Assam
Rev. Sister Superior, Little Flower School, Dibrugarh, Assam
Rev. Sister Superior, St. Mary's School, Dibrugarh, Assam

Kindly confirm,

Yours Faithfully,

Chairman of Tirap
Catholic Church Association
P. O. Borduria
Arunachal Pradesh

■ ■ ■

To,
   The DC
   Khonsa, Tirap District
   Arunachal Pradesh.

Subject: Reservation of Circuit House

Sir,
Kindly reserve 4 (four) rooms at Khonsa Circuit House for the 1st and 2nd of Aug '79 for the Bishop of Dibrugarh/Tezpur and other Church dignitaries.
   I will be much obliged if confirmation is intimated at an early date.

Yours faithfully,

(Wanglat Lowangcha)

■ ■ ■

GOVERNMENT OF ARUNACHAL PRADESH
OFFICE OF THE DEPUTY COMMISSIONER
TIRAP DISTRICT
KHONSA

NO ENG 12/78/116
Dated Khonsa the 23rd July '79

To,
   The Assistant Engineer
   Khonsa Building Sub-Division
   Khonsa

Subject: Reservation of rooms in circuit house Khonsa

Sir,
I am forwarding herewith the original letter No. DR-VIP/78-79/I of 23/7/79 received from Shri Wanglat Lowangcha, General Secretary, and PPA for consideration.

Yours faithfully,

Dated:- 23rd July 1979

For DC of Tirap Dist., Khonsa

Memo No ENG 12/79/116

Copy to: Shri Wanglat Lowangcha, Genl. Secy., PPA, For information with reference to the above

■ ■ ■

To,
 The Asst. Engineer,
 Khonsa Sub-Division,
 Tirap Dist.,
 Arunachal Pradesh.

Subject: Temporary Electric Connection

Sir,
We will be grateful to you if you kindly give us temporary electrification at Borduria "HUM WANG" ceremony for three days i.e. from 31st July to 2nd Aug '79. We will need four tube lights,

two mercury lamps. Six bulb points and two plug points. We are willing to deposit the regular security fees.

We will be thankful if you kindly confirm.

Yours faithfully,

Dated:- 24th July 1979

(Thinhak Dada)
GPM
Borduria
Chairman TCA

■ ■ ■

OFFICE OF THE ASSISTANT ENGINEER, KHONSA BUILDING SUB DIVISION

NO KW/79/27

Dated Khonsa the 25th July '79

To
    The DC
    Tirap Dist., Khonsa

Subject: Reservation of the Circuit House

Sir,
With reference to the above this is to inform you that rooms have already been reserved for two officers of NEITC Gauhati as requisitioned by Deputy Director of Industries, Khonsa from

28/7/79 to 4/8/79 vide his No. DIC/135/79-80 dt. 24/7/79, your requisition has been received later on. The available other three rooms have been reserved for Shri Wanglat Lowangcha, Secretary of PPA.

Yours faithfully,
Assistant Engineer,
Khonsa Bldg Sub-Divn.

Dated, Khonsa the 25th July '79

■ ■ ■

GOVERNMENT OF ARUNACHAL PRADESH
OFFICE OF THE DEPUTY COMMISSIONER, TIRAP DISTRICT, KHONSA

Memo No. CA 129/79/19

Dated the 30th July '79

Whereas a controversy has cropped regarding the proposed visit of the Bishops and other Roman Catholic priests to Borduria village in connection with the blessing ceremony of the Roman Catholic Church there on the 2nd August next, the undersigned regrets his inability to issue any Inner Line Pass to them at this stage.

(J. M. Syiem)
Deputy Commissioner,
Tirap District, Khonsa

To,

    Shri Wanglat Lowangcha
    With reference to his application
    Shri Chanlang Mongchan

■ ■ ■

GOVERNMENT OF ARUNACHAL PRADESH
OFFICE OF THE DEPUTY COMMISSIONER, TIRAP DISTRICT, KHONSA

Memo No. CA 129/79/22

Dt. Khonsa, 31st July '79

In continuation to this office letter No. CA 129/79/22 dated the 30th instant, Shri Wanglat Lowangcha is hereby informed that an Inner Line Pass for the Roman Catholic Bishops and priests has been issued. In this connection, however, I would like to say here that from what we find, there is a rift in Borduria village. I would, therefore, like to have a meeting with the Chief and the people concerned about this so that the unity of the village is maintained.

Deputy Commissioner
Khonsa

Document 40:

GOVERNMENT OF ARUNACHAL PRADESH OFFICE OF THE DEPUTY COMMISSIONER: TIRAP: KHONSA

Memo No. CA 128/79/6

Dated Khonsa the 20th Aug '79

Shri Wanglat Lowangcha
Borduria.

It is seen that a number of persons have been converted to Roman Catholic on the 2nd instant when the church building at Borduria was blessed on that day, in which two Bishops and some Roman Catholic Priests were also present.

In this connection your attention is drawn to Sec 1 of the Arunachal Freedom of Religion Action 1978 in which it is laid down that the fact of such conversion must be intimated to the DC. No such intimation has been received. You are, therefore, hereby directed to send a list of such persons converted to Roman Catholic on the 2nd instant, showing their names, father's (or husband's name in the case of married woman), their age and villages. This intimation may please be sent within a fortnight of the issue of this.

Sd/-
(P. C. Das) EAC
For Deputy Commissioner,
Khonsa.

■ ■ ■

To,
> The Deputy Commissioner
> Khonsa, Tirap Dist.
> Arunachal Pradesh.

Ref: Your letter No. Memo No. CA128/79/6

Dated Khonsa the 20th Aug '79

Sir,
I humbly would like to submit the following few points for your kind future course of action.

1. It is with regret to know that you and Mr. S. N. Mitra, Extra Assistant Commissioner have been sending Memos to me. Please note that I am not working under you or your office for you to send me Memos. All letters addressed to me may kindly be sent in an official form. If in case I am accused in any crime it should also have a proper form. Please remember that I am the General Secretary of a state opposition party, whose party has been officially recognized and registered by the Chief Election Commissioner, Govt. of India. Moreover the Speaker of the Arunachal Pradesh Assembly has recognized our party as the Official Opposition Party in the Assembly. I therefore request you to have the courtesy to address a letter properly.
2. In case I have corresponded any letter with you as the Chairman of Arunachal Christian Action Committee, kindly reply accordingly under the name and style of the office I hold. I have been elected as the Chairman of

ACAC amidst four (4) Hon'ble MPs and different Church leaders of N. E. India. I'm therefore duly recognized by the Christians of N. E. and Arunachal Pradesh as their leader.

3. I am surprised at your understanding of the Arunachal Freedom of Religion Act '78. I don't think there is any Act known as Arunachal Pradesh Freedom of Religion Action 1978. If I am not mistaken you must be referring to "Arunachal Pradesh Freedom of Religion Act, 1978."

4. While drawing my attention to Sec 1 of the APFR Act '78, I could only find that this small section deals only with the title of the Act, its jurisdiction and when shall it come into force. If I am not mistaken I think you are referring to Section 5, Part (1).

5. Now if you are referring to Section 5, part (1) of APFR Act '78, I am here to inform you that I do not know who took Baptism. It will only be known to the seven (7) priests who performed the baptism ceremony and by the persons who took baptism. I was only a spectator as were many officers who were sitting on the platform while baptism took place inside the pandal (temporary hall). I was not an instrument to their baptism; therefore you are requested kindly to correspond with the concerned people.

The above few points are for your kind information.

Yours faithfully

(Wanglat Lowang)

■ ■ ■

GOVERNMENT OF ARUNACHAL PRADESH
OFFICE OF THE DEPUTY COMMISSIONER: TIRAP
DISTRICT: KHONSA

NO. CA.128/79/21

Dated Khonsa, the 17th Sep '79

To
    Shri Wanglat Lowangcha
    Borduria Village.

With reference to your letter dated 25th August last, I am to say that you had applied for Inner Line Pass for the Bishops and Roman Catholic priests who came to your village on the 2nd August last. It is, therefore, obvious that you are quite aware you had taken part indirectly in the conversion of people to Christianity on the 2nd August last in Borduria village. Hence an intimation is required to be sent to the undersigned of the fact of such conversion as provided u/s 5 (1) of the Arunachal freedom of Religion Act, 1978.

    Please, therefore, arrange to send the same accordingly by the 30th inst. positively.

(J. M. Syiem)
Deputy Commissioner,
Tirap District,
Khonsa.

■ ■ ■

KHONSA, the 27th September, 1979

To,
   The Deputy Commissioner,
   Tirap Dist.,
   Khonsa.

Sir,
   Ref: Your memo No. CA 128/79/21
   Dated 17.9.79

While acknowledging the receipt of your above, I am pained to note that in spite of the clarifications of my stand of the subject contained in my letter dt. 25.8.1979, I have been dragged into the controversy by repetition of the charges and thereby put to unnecessary harassment.

As I now feel and understand, this is a calculated attempt by an unholy alliance to frustrate my social career by throwing allegations against me. I strongly deplore the malicious designs with which things are being hatched up and fabricated against me by some persons of authority with vested interests. Anyway, I cannot surely be made answerable to anything I am not concerned with as I have already pointed out in my previous letter.

As to my arranging the Inner Line Pass for the Bishop, I did it in my capacity as the Chairman of the ACAC, as a routine work and questioning my authority to do so amounts to infringement of my civic rights.

Lastly, I would request your good self not to address me any further correspondence on the subject, the need of which I believe, no longer exists.

Yours faithfully,

Sd/- Wanglat Lowangcha

■ ■ ■

ARUNACHAL CHRISTIAN ACTION COMMITTEE
C/O Bishop's House—Phone 181
Dibrugarh

To,
   The Hon'ble Lt. Governor,
   Arunachal Pradesh
   Itanagar

Sub:- Undue harassment by District Authority, Khonsa, on Shri Wanglat Lowangcha & other innocent villagers of Borduria village, Tirap Dist., A. P.

Sir,
I have the honour to draw your attention to the following few lines on the above subject to appraise your good self on how people in Arunachal are harassed for reasons best known to the authorities.

On 20th Aug '79 I received a Memo from the D. C., Khonsa alleging that I took part in the conversion of some people of

Borduria village, Tirap Dist. when on 2.8.79, the Bishop and others during their visit blessed the local church. As it was a mischievous attempt on the part of the District Authority based on fictitious reports and aimed at lowering my social status, I replied on 25.8.79 clarifying my stand on the matter. It seems that the D. C., Khonsa was not satisfied with my said reply and wrote to me again on 17.9.79 demanding that I should supply the names of converts as well as how they were converted. I am therefore very much perturbed at the way the matter is pursued against me by the authority, with possible ultimate object to make me criminally liable for things that are beyond my control and I am unconcerned with. This is not the only example of high handedness of the District Authority, Khonsa. Some 21 persons have been illegally summoned to appear in court in a proceeding U/S 108 Cr.P.C., the charges reading "Discriminating religion into sect. of Borduria and attempting conversion, etc." which is all fictitious and frivolous. Also there are some more cases raised against the poor villagers under different charges. Some of them have been charged under the provisions of the APFR Act, 1978, whereby I dare say, that the Act has not been implemented properly but misused grossly to the greatest prejudice of the people at large.

All these go to show that there is a clear conspiracy against me to malign me in the eyes of the public as well as to make me legally answerable for nothing. And the poor people who are quite ignorant of what is going on around are unnecessarily dragged into a controversial matter with some purpose and ulterior motives behind.

I therefore, bring the above to the notice of your good self seeking and soliciting justice and hope that this will be looked into your good self sympathetically and impartially.

Yours faithfully,

(Wanglat Lowangcha)
Vill. Borduria
Tirap Dist., AP.

Copy to:
The Hon'ble Chief Minister, AP, Itanagar
Shri Bakin Pertin, President, UPPA, Itanagar
Local MLA for kind information and necessary action

■ ■ ■

SECRETARY TO LIEUTENANT GOVERNOR
ARUNACHAL PRADESH
ITANAGAR—791 111

No. LG.2/79 (Vol. II)

Dated 6th Oct '79

To,
Shri Wanglat Lowangcha,
Village Borduria,
Tirap District,
Arunachal Pradesh.

Sub: Undue harassment by District Authority, Khonsa on Shri Wanglat Lowangcha & other innocent villagers of Borduria village, Tirap Dist., A. P.

Sir,
I am directed to acknowledge receipt of your letter dated 29th Sept '79 addressed to the Lt. Governor, on the subject noted above and to say that your letter has been endorsed to the Chief Secretary for necessary action.

Yours faithfully,

(T. P. Khaund)
Secretary to the Lt. Governor
Arunachal Pradesh

Document 41:

RANGSON PRESERVATION AND PROTECTION COMMITTEE
NOCTE RELIGION AND CULTURE IN DANGER

WANGLIN LOWANGDONG
PRESIDENT

WE, the Noctes of the Tirap District of Arunachal Pradesh are deeply shocked to learn that very recently some Catholic Priests came from Dibrugarh and other places to our Borduria village near Khonsa to convert our innocent people residing in that village by adopting (1) Inducement (2) Fraud (3) Force, which are illegal according to Arunachal Pradesh Freedom of Religion Act, 1978.

As per Govt. Circular No. CA/24/28/43 dated 16.10.78 issued by the DC, Khonsa, Dist. Tirap, construction of any other place of worship other than 'Traditional place of worship' is prohibited.

We wonder how permission was obtained to construct a church at Borduria village in spite of strong protest made by the villagers including the Chief of Borduria; the church was formally inaugurated by the foreign Missionaries on August 2, 1979. It is also surprising to note that how the Inner Line Permit was made available to them by the Administration.

It seems that the entire incident was pre-planned. So there must be something wrong somewhere in the local administrative system. Otherwise, how could they have obtained permission to construct a church, and an Inner Line Permit for doing the greatest harm to the innocent people by destroying our old age religion and culture? We have brought to the notice of the Deputy Commissioner by submitting a Memorandum on 7.9.79, with a request to take immediate action.

In connection with the mischief that has already been done to the people of our Borduria village in the Dist. of Tirap, we would like to remind all our brothers that we are the descendents of the great king saint Narottam. Our tradition says that some time in the 17th century, Latha Khunbao, the Nocte king dreamt the preceptor of his previous birth and floated two bamboo pipes, one of gold and one of silver, down the Namsang river to trace his Guru or preceptor. As the king and his subjects were following the course of the bamboo pipes, these pipes came to place called Merbil near Naharkatiya where the saint Shri Ram Ata stayed with his disciples. The personal attendants of Shri Ram Ata saw and tried to touch the pipes but they drifted away. On being informed when Shri Ram Ata himself came and prayed to the pipes offering betel, they came within his reach. Then when King Latha Khunbao and his people prayed for initiation, Shri Ram Dev at first refused as he wanted to test. When a play on *"Kalia Daman"* was going on, Shri Ram Ata appeared in guise of an ordinary man with torn and dirty clothes. Being a true devotee, Khunbao could immediately recognize his Guru Shri Dev. At this Shri Ram Dev was very pleased and initiated the king Latha with all his followers. From that day Latha was known as Narottam (the best among men) and became a devout of Shri Ram Dev. Since that time, the Nocte have been practicing Nocteism.

The Guru Shri Ram Ata and disciple Narottam have been in intimate even in death for they died on the same day. The fact that the flames which from both the pyre mingled atop the pyres thus signifying their blessed union in life and death is still remembered among the Noctes.

Dear brothers, if we ponder deeply over the story of our saint Narottam, will it not be an act of sacrilege, if we fore seek the grand religion of our forefathers, being dumped into all sorts of allurements and false propaganda? Does not in our vain flow the pure blood of our great saint Narottam? Is it not our sacred duty to be conscious of this and to prove loyal by our thoughts and deeds to his great teachings? Should we not feel proud of his glorious heritage and go from door to door, village to village to propagate the teachings of our great saint thus jeopardizing all ministers attempt at conversation by the wicked Missionaries. In all these noble efforts of ours, we will not only have the blessing of our great saint Narottam, we will also have the good will and support of all the people of Arunachal Pradesh and of all the other people of other states of India, who are keen on preserving our ancient religion and culture.

In conclusion, we demand an immediate enquiry into all that has happened in Borduria village and urge upon the Govt. of Arunachal Pradesh and the Home Ministry of the Govt. of India to take more strict measures, so that no Inner Line Permit is issued to any foreign Missionaries or Priests or Pastors by way of safeguarding our old age religion and culture, in the larger interest of the solidarity, unity and national integration.

JAI HIND.

> WANG LIN LOWANG DONG
> CHIEF OF BORDURIA ON BEHALF
> OF NOCTE PEOPLE AND PRESIDENT
> RANGSOM PRESERVATION AND
> PROTECTION COMMITTEE.

September 16, 1979

■■■

From: M. Abdur Rahman,
    Advocate, Bar Association,
    Dibrugarh.

To: Shri Wanglin Lowangdong,
    President, Rangsom Preservation and Protection Committee,
    P.O. Borduria (via Khonsa)
    Tirap Dist.
    Arunachal Pradesh.

Dear Sir,
Under instructions from my client Shri Wanglat Lowangcha of Borduria village, I give you notice as under:-
    On 6.8.79 you addressed a letter to the DC, Tirap Dist., Khonsa, wherein you have raised serious allegations against my

said client. You have alleged amongst many others that my client took leading part in conversion of people to Christianity in Borduria Village which is utterly false and aimed at damaging the image of my client in the Nocte society as a social leader of high repute. In fact, your allegations are sufficiently provocative to spread disharmony and dissension amongst the innocent, peace loving Nocte community, thereby creating tension in the village as evidenced from your pamphlets captioned "Nocte Religion and Culture in danger" published in your name on 16.9.79.

Various other false and fictitious claims have also been made by you before the District Authority implicating my client and his men taking advantage of his silence over your malafide activities.

You are, therefore, hereby requested not to indulge further in such unsocial acts against my client for the greater interest of the Nocte people in general and Borduria villagers in particular. In case of your failure to do so, I have instructions to take appropriate legal actions against you and in such event you will be solely liable for all consequences please note.

Yours faithfully,

Copy to: the Deputy Commissioner, Tirap Dist. Khonsa for favour of his information and to take necessary steps in the matter for maintenance of peace in the villagers against undue harassment and possible victimization for nothing. This has reference to the various complaints lodged by Shri Wanglin Lowangdong and at his instance, by others, some of which have already come up for hearing in the courts at Khonsa.

Document 43:

NORTH EAST INDIA JOINT ACTION COMMITTEE FOR RELIGIOUS FREEDOM SHILLONG, AUGUST 20, 1979

In the General Assembly of the Christian leaders (North-East India) that met at Shillong on June 29, 1979, it was decided that Tadar Taniang be entrusted with the task of collecting such documents as might be necessary for taking legal action against persecutors in Arunachal Pradesh. He was mainly to visit the Christian areas of Subansiri and Siang.

Here is a report of Tadar Taniang's assignment:
"I was asked by the NEI Action Committee for Religious Freedom to collect incriminating documents to take legal action against those who were persecuting Christians in Arunachal Pradesh. I visited the following areas.

30.6.79: I left Shillong and reached Tezpur.

Halted at Tezpur to find out if the file of Mr. Taram Nelam (he had been persecuted) contained any relevant papers. But his file had not been given to Rev. M. A. Z. Rolston by Dr. C. L. Rema. I sent a telegram to Rev. Rolston requesting him to send the file to Fr. Thomas, Don Bosco Technical School, Shillong.

Left Tezpur for North Lakhimpur

Left North Lakhimpur and reached Hawa village. There I met Mr. Ter Tana.

Left Hawa village and reached Yazali. I talked with the Christians there. On the same day I left for Ziro. From there I visited Joram, Talo, Sete and other villages.

Left Ziro for Pasighat.

10.7.79: Left North Lakhimpur and reached Likhabali. I stayed with a pastor that night. I fell sick and the Christians looked after me.

11.7.79: Left Likhabali and visited Sipi village. I met Mr. T. Tiba, one of the pastors and spent the night there.

12.7.79: Left Sipi village and reached Sille and proceeded to Pasighat. It was raining heavily and I travelled on foot with bag and baggage. Communication lines are still very poor in many parts of Arunachal Pradesh.

15.7.79: Left Pasighat for North Lakhimpur. On the way I was nearly hit by a stone thrown by *goondas*, but God saved my life. The tour had been very troublesome and dangerous.

16.7.79: Left North Lakhimpur and reached Itanagar and visited Ganga village.

19.7.79: Left Itanagar and reached Ziro

25.7.79: Left Ziro and reached Shillong on 26.7.79 where I was followed by a group of S. I. B. and S. B. men."

In Shillong, Mr. Tadar Taniang met Mr. M. S. Jahrin, advocate, along with the two Secretaries of the Action Committee. After studying the documents carefully, they found that most files (Including that of Mr. Taram Nelam which had been sent to Rev. Rolston) contained only true copies of documents. At this stage only original copies would be required. Original copies of letters from the DC or other Government Officers ordering the demolition of churches or cessation of construction of churches, etc. would be most welcome from any readers of this letter. We can return the document after making photostat copies of the same. Kindly oblige.

It was decided that a defamation case be filed in the Sessions Court at Ziro by Mr. Taram Nelam or some other complainant against Mr. Takar Techi, who sent a blasphemous memorandum to the President. Mr. Tadar Taniang would follow up the case. Meanwhile efforts should continue to collect adequate documents for taking up a case against demolition orders of churches.

Letters are being sent to the Chief Ministers of North-Eastern States who are due to meet in Shillong shortly, requesting them to exert their pressure for the repeal of the Arunachal Pradesh Freedom of Religion Bill Act and the appointment of a Commission to enquire into the allegations of harassment of Christians in the Union Territories.

We are sending you this brief account to keep you informed of what is being done to follow up the decisions of the meeting that was held in Shillong on June 29, 1979.

Fr. Thomas Menamparampil
Mr. P. B. M. Basaiawmoit
(Joint Secretaries)

Document 44:

TIRAP BAPTIST CHURCH COUNCIL
SONKING, P. O. MIAO, 792122
ARUNACHAL PRADESH, INDIA

AUGUST 22, 1979

Wanglat Lowangcha
President, ACAC
Borduria P. O.
Arunachal Pradesh.

Dear Wanglat,

Congratulations for the success of your Church opening. I couldn't come there as Jugli and self went to Nagaland for special duty.

Angon Ratan had written that in discussions with Tadar Taniang, they fixed ACAC meeting on 17th Sep. to discuss possibility of filing a legal suit by Tajin Tamut of Doring village a man who lost his W. R. C. field for his faith.

I left this to you for final decisions. From my end unless there is progressive news about the proposed cases already by Taniang there is no point of searching for so many legal suits.

The call for ACAC meeting I leave to you for decision whether to held or not to be held.

Sincerely yours,
L. M. Yanger,
Secy., ACAC

■ ■ ■

ARUNACHAL CHRISTIAN ACTION COMMITTEE
C/O BISHOP'S HOUSE—PHONE: 181
DIBRUGARH

Mr. L. M. Yanger,
Secretary, ACAC
Sonking Village,
Tirap Dist., A.P.

Dear Yanger,

Thank you for your kind letter. Sorry I was not quick in replying it. I have been very busy trying to sort out things for our people. Yanger I too think we should immediately have a meeting of the ACAC. Say on the 17th Sep '79 as fixed by Angon and Co. After the opening of the Church and some baptism L. G. and C. M. has visited Khonsa and they have encouraged the anti-Christian group to counter with full Government backing. L. G. himself has publicly made a statement that he will instruct the D. C. Khonsa to fully implement the APFR Act '78. We must be prepared for any eventualities. Therefore I request you to kindly inform all our members to come for the meeting at Dibrugarh. Tomorrow I will be going to Dibrugarh. There I will inform the Bishop to kindly allow us to use his place both for the meeting and those who want to stay.

    I am also enclosing two cheques for you to sign and send to Fr. Joseph, Secy. to the Bishop, Bishop House, Dibrugarh. One cheque is for me which I have taken from him and the other is for the office Secy.

Yours sincerely,
(Wanglat Lowangcha)

Document 45:

NORTH-EAST INDIA JOINT ACTION COMMITTEE FOR RELIGIOUS FREEDOM SHILLONG

North-east India Joint Action Committee for Religious Freedom is an inter-denominational body set up in 1979 for safeguarding the Constitutional rights of the Christian Community in North-East India.

In a meeting of the NEIJAC for Religious Freedom held in Shillong on August 25th under the Chairmanship of Archbishop Hubert D'Rosario to study the present campaign in the press against particular churches and the functionaries of various Christian's denominations, the following resolutions were unanimously adopted:

The Committee takes a serious view of the current situation in which a number of public leaders and a section of the press have been making highly inflammatory statements with regard to the Christian activities and undertakings in North-East India with no other possible intention than that of whipping up communal frenzy:

Functionaries of Christian churches have been accused of misuse of funds and subversive activities.

Individual churches have been accused of fomenting disaffection and promoting violent and secessionist movements.

The Committee feels convinced that such propaganda against Christian leaders and undertakings is being organized with the deliberate intention of discrediting the entire Christian endeavour in North-East India for the following reasons:

Virulent accusations are substantiated by no convincing evidence

Baseless allegations are given in headlines in the press. Christian answers to them are not usually published at all or are confined to the footnotes. This is evidently done with the malicious intention of leaving behind a negative image of Christians. And that, in spite of the fact not a single one of the allegations has been proved true.

There seems to be absolutely no consideration for the sentiments of 25 lakhs Christians in North-East India who have been thoroughly humiliated and deeply disillusioned.

The Committee fails to understand in what sense this calumny of Christians is not a COMMUNAL OFFENCE. Persons guilty of this crime will have to take full responsibility for the estrangement of religious communities among themselves and the emotional alienation of millions of hearts giving rise to mounting tension and deep bitterness. This irresponsible manner of speaking and acting renders meaningless subsequent sermonization on emotional integration of various social and religious groups. The very fabric of our nation is being daily undermined.

The Committee protests against the idea that Christian priests, evangelists or pastors are working in a particular area or carrying out a particular task because of any concession granted to them by anyone, on the contrary, they perform their duty in exercise of their civic rights which no authority stands by the Constitution can take away. The Christian community is ready to defend its Constitutional rights, and any attempt at curtailing them shall be resisted.

The Committee resents the dubious use of the word "Missionary" in the present context, frequently qualified by the objective "Foreign." It feels certain that it is done with the mischievous intention of arousing suspicion and making light of the dynamism of the Indian Christian Community that has a history of 2,000 years in the country.

The Committee is deeply distressed over recent happenings in Arunachal Pradesh, esp. in Tirap Dist., where reportedly several churches have been pulled down, Christians have been arrested and others are facing arrest—all in the name of the much discredited Arunachal Pradesh Freedom of Religion Act, 1978.

The Committee condemns every form of violence as contrary to the spirit of the Gospel. It expresses it eagerness to cooperate with every legitimate authority and with all persons of good will in a common effort for creating an atmosphere of peace and mutual trust in North-East India. But it feels that such an atmosphere shall remain a remote dream as long as the leaders of any religious society and even the very societies themselves are being maligned by public leaders and journalists. Irreparable damage has already been done. Everyone's earnest effort is required to remove mistrust and fear from the hearts of people and restore mutual confidence.

Archbishop Hubert D'Rosario
(Joint Chairman)
Archbishop's House,
Shillong—793003
Mr. P. B. M. Basaiawmoit
(Joint Secretary)
Hony. Adviser
Village Defence Organization
Mawkhar, Shillong 793001

Bishop D. D. Pradhan
(Joint Chairman)
Bishop's Kuti,
Shillong 793001
Fr. Thomas Menaparampil
(Joint Secretary)
Don Bosco Tech. School
Shillong 793003

Regd.: A/D

Document 46:

Dt. 26.9.79

In the Court of Shri Harbans Singh,
Judicial Mgt. (I) Khonsa.

Case No. 49/79 u/s 108 Cr.P.C.

Deputy Commissioner, Tirap Dist.: 1st Party
                    VS
Wangsun Medam and 20 others: 2nd Party

The second party above respectfully showed:

That the 2nd party have received summons U/S 113 Cr.P.C. to appear before your honour today and to show cause, why they should not be required to enter into a bond of Rs.500/- each.

That non-compliance of an order as such makes one legally liable and hence, although the 2nd party has no knowledge of allegations, that cover, against them, they appear in this court today in person and through their Lawyer.

That a proceeding U/S 108 Cr.P.C. stipulates an order to be made in writing setting forth the substance of any information received by the court, etc. If the court deems it necessary to require any person to show cause, as provided U/S 111 Cr.P.C. and absence of such an order which is equivalent to a charge sheet in warrant cases vitals the proceedings being prejudicial to the party concerned and the court in such an event loses its jurisdiction.

That an order U/S/Cr.P.C. accompanied by a copy of the police report must be served on the parties concerned and always precede any action U/S 113 Cr.P.C.

That S.114 Cr.P.C. provides service of summons U/S 113 Cr.P.C. to be accompanied by a copy of order U/S 111 Cr.P.C. as a measure if emergency only and violation thereof renders the proceedings invalid.

That show-case to bind down tantamount to interference with liberty of the person proceeded against without valid grounds and proceedings as such being illegal are liable to be dropped.

That this court has inherent power to drop the proceedings at any stage.

It is praised that your honour would be pleased to carefully examine the legal aspects and implications and upon your satisfaction, drop the proceedings and exempt the 2nd party from liability whatsoever and for this act of kindness, etc.

* The show cause notice was issued to the above twenty leaders for accepting the Christian faith at the behest of the anti-Christian complaints. This clearly indicates how law can be twisted to punish Christians in a secular India.

Document 47:

Dt.: 26.9.79

To,
  The Deputy Commissioner,
  Tirap Dist., Khonsa, A. P.
  Ref: - Realization of bail amount in cash

Sir,
I beg to inform you that I stood bail for Shri Khamsuam Pongtey for Rs. 500/- (Rupees Five Hundred) only, in a case U/S 3 of APFR Act, 1978 pending in the court of Shri S. R. Sarkar, Magistrate and

the O.C. Khonsa realized Rs. 500/- (Rupees Five Hundred) only, in cash from me on 24.9.79 against issue of a receipt which shows that the amount was realized on behalf of the Judicial Magistrate Khonsa.

The amount was paid by me for fear of torture and insult on the hand of Police, against my will but such realization is illegal.

I therefore, request your good self to cause an enquiry into the matter, arrange for the refund of the amount to me and to take necessary steps as deemed fit and proper against the delinquent officer.

Yours faithfully,

Sd/- Chagan Medam

* Chagan Medam's bail deposit for Khamsuam Pongtey. (Khamsuam was a traditional faith healer who did not convert to Christianity but supported the Christians of Borduria village. The Government, not knowing this fact, falsely accused Khansuam U/S 3 of APFR Act, 1978.)

Document 48:

The letters below show us how the Government of Arunachal Pradesh is discriminating against the Christians.

The first letter refuses permission to Bishop Joseph Mittathany of Tezpur Diocese, under whose spiritual jurisdiction Arunachal falls, to enter the territory to minister to the spiritual needs of his flock for Christmas. We read in Mother Teresa's letter to our prime minister how Rama Krishna Mission members are given full access to the same territory for the same purpose for which they deny the Christian priest, nuns, and bishop to enter.

The second letter directs the deputy commissioner of Tirap District to release immediately 600 bags of cement to build a Buddhist temple. Is this just?

The third letter warns that no religious places of worship other than those of indigenous faiths can be constructed in Arunachal Pradesh.

The next two letters clearly express that the Government has come to know from reliable sources that one church was being built in Khonsa village and that it should be demolished immediately.

* Article published by ACAC in 1979.

■ ■ ■

Letter 1

GOVERNMENT OF ARUNACHAL PRADESH
OFFICE OF THE DEPUTY COMMISSIONER: SUBANSIRI DISTRICT

N.C. 27900/262

Dated Ziro, the 27th Nov '78

To
    The Rev. Fr. Job Appathara
    Catholic Church
    North Lakhimpur (Assam)

Sir,
I am in receipt of your letter dated 4th Oct '78 in connection with the issue of Inner Line Permits to you and Bishop Rt. Rev.

Joseph Mittathany for conducting religious services in the villages around Ziro during the last week of December next.

In this connection, I am to inform you that as per Government's instruction (Resolution of the Union Cabinet of 26th May, 1953) no religious priests belonging to any community, which includes Christian Missionary also, are allowed to enter Arunachal Pradesh for preaching of religion. Since the proposed visit of the Bishop is for conducting religious services, it is regretted that no Inner Line Permits can be issued to him.

Yours faithfully,

Sd/- (B. S. Kharayat)
(Dt. 27-11-78)
Deputy Commissioner,
Subansiri District, Ziro

■ ■ ■

Letter 2

GOVERNMENT OF ARUNACHAL PRADESH
LIEUTENANT GOVERNOR SECRETARIAT: ITANAGAR

NO. CA. 24/78/43

Date Itanagar the 5th Oct '78

From: Shri T. P. Khaund
    Secretary to Lt. Governor
    Itanagar

To: The Secretary
    Supply and Transport, Govt. of A. P.
    Shillong

Sub:- Release of cement from public sale quota

Sir,

I am directed to enclose herewith a copy of an application from Shri Samchom Ngemu, General Secretary, Aangsa Singpho Cultural Society, P. O. Namchik, Tirap District, Arunachal Pradesh about release of 600 bags of cement required for the construction of a Buddhist temple at Kharsang.

The Buddhist temple at Kharsang is very important project and has to be completed expeditiously. I am, therefore, directed to request you to kindly instruct the Deputy Commissioner, Tirap District, Khonsa to release 600 bags of cement from public sale quota to the Tangsa Singpho Cultural Society as early as possible.

Encl. as above

Yours faithfully,
Sd/- T. P. Khaund
SECRETARY

Memo No. LG. 11/77 (Part II)

Dt. Itanagar the 5th Oct '78

Copy to:-

1. The Deputy Commissioner, Tirap District, Khonsa along with a copy of application from the General Secretary, Tangsa

Singpho Cultural Society for information. He is requested kindly to arrange 600 bags of cement to the Society for the construction of a proposed Buddhist temple at Kharsang.
2. Shri Samchom Ngemu, General Secretary, Tangsa Singpho Cultural Society, P.O. Namchik, Kharsang, Tirap District, for information.

Sd/- T. P. Khaund
SECRETARY

■ ■ ■

Letter 3

GOVERNMENT OF ARUNACHAL PRADESH
OFFICE OF THE DEPUTY COMMISSIONER: TIRAP
DISTRICT: KHONSA

NO.CA. 24/78/43

Dated Khonsa the 16th Oct '78

This is for general information for all concerned that no house of worship, other than those in respect of the traditional faith, will be allowed to be constructed without the prior permission of the Government.

If such houses of worship are constructed without Government's permission they will be demolished without any liability to the Government.

Sd/- J. M. Syiem
Deputy Commissioner,
Tirap District, Khonsa.

■ ■ ■

Letter 4

GOVERNMENT OF ARUNACHAL PRADESH
OFFICE OF THE EXTRA ASSTT. COMMISSIONER:
TIRAP DISTRICT: MIAO

No. M/O. M/CON-7/75-78/442-45

Dated, Miao, the 9th Nov '78

To 1. The GB
2. The Secretary (TBCC), Songking

Sir,
Enclosed please find herewith the copy of office memo No. CA/24/78/43 dt. 16.10.78 from the Deputy Commissioner, Khonsa for favour of your information and strict compliance.

Yours faithfully,

Sd/- B. Baruah 9/11
Extra Assistant Commissioner, Miao

■ ■ ■

Letter 5

URGENT
GOVT. OF ARUNACHAL PRADESH
OFFICE OF THE EXTRA ASSISTANT COMMISSIONER:
MIAO

No. M/CON-7/75-78/12268

Miao the 22nd Nov '78

NOTICE

It is to remind you that construction of any religious temple/church other than those of indigenous faiths has strictly been prohibited as per order of the Deputy Commissioner, Khonsa which was forwarded to you vide this official letter No. M/CON 7/75/461-39 dated 25/10/78. It is learnt from reliable sources that one church is being constructed in your village. Please ensure that no construction on any church/temple be taken up in your village and if any structure has meanwhile been erected, the same should be immediately demolished as per order of the Deputy Commissioner, Khonsa. A copy of the letter No. CA-24/78/43 dated 16th October, 1978 received from the Deputy Commissioner, Khonsa is also enclosed herewith again for your immediate compliance.

Please confirm action taken on the matter failing which necessary action will be taken as per law.

Encl:
As stated

> Sd/- B. Baruah 22/11/78
> Extra Assistant Commissioner,
> Miao Sub-division: Miao

To
The GB,
Songking village

Document 49:

GOVT. OF ARUNACHAL PRADESH
OFFICE OF THE CIRCLE OFFICER: TIRAP DIST.:
MANMAO

NO. MOC-7/86-87/391-93

> Dt. Manmao the 20th Oct '87

To,
    Shri Wangkum Ronrang, Pastor
    Shri Hangrey Ronrang
    Shri Hangnem Ronrang
    Camp Lungchang Village

It is reported that you are carrying out preaching and baptizing people against their will.

You are hereby directed not to carry out such activities in future and not to move around without permission.

Sd /-
(L. Yomgam) CO
Manmao, Tirap Dist.

Document 50:

Missionaries Are Persona Non Grata in Arunachal Pradesh

The secret message (confirmed) vide letter No. Conf/32/88/15002 dated Nahar Lagun 29th June '88 reads as follows:

2790 of 23/6/88 (.) HENCEFORTH NO CHRISTIAN MISSIONARY IS TO BE PERMITTED TO ENTER OUR DISTRICT FROM ANY POINT (.) ALSO NO INNER LINE PASS IN RESPECT TO MISSIONARIES ISSUED BY ANY OTHER THAN DC ZIRO UNDER HIS OWN SIGNATURE IS TO BE HONOURED BY CHECK POST POLICE (.) CHECK POST AT BANDERDAWA/BALIJAN/DOIMUKH AND KIMIN MAY BE INSTRUCTED ACCORDINGLY (.) VIGOROUS CHECKING Of ALL PASSES OF ALL CHRISTIAN MISSIONARIES IS FOUND WITHOUT VALID PASS HE MAY BE DEALT WITH STRICTLY (.) ALL TO ACK (.)

* Such confidential and secret directives are issued to district administrators for complian

Early Church in Arunachal Pradesh

Church which was destroyed in 1978.
Home Minister H M Patel called it a kutcha church

Crucifix gifted to Wanglat by Fr. Rubio of Shillong in 1977 which was installed in the first consecrated Catholic Church in Borduria

The first Catholic Church of Arunachal Pradesh in Borduria officially consecrated in 1979

The first 'pucca' Catholic Church of Arunachal Pradesh which was inaugurated in Borduria by Mother Teresa and consecrated by Archbishop Thomas in 1993

The Catholic Church in Borduria built to replace the first thatched roof and bamboo walled church

Cathedral of Miao Diocese, East Arunachal Pradesh

Cathedral of Itanagar Diocese, West Arunachal Pradesh

St Mary's Catholic Church, Itanagar

Baptist Church at Naharlagun. Naharlagun was the first capital of Arunachal Pradesh where major decisions were taken to persecute Christians of Arunachal Pradesh

Baptist Church in Nirjuli Town where persecutions were at their peak between 1973-1990

Christian Revival Church, Itanagar (exterior), the first airconditioned church of Arunachal Pradesh

Christian Revival Church, Itanagar (interior), the first airconditioned church of Arunachal Pradesh

First Mother Teresa Home of the Missionaries of Charity, Itanagar

Mother Teresa Home of the Missionaries of Charity at Borduria

Shrine of St Anthony in Borduria where miracles take place and prayers of believers are answered

Mother Teresa being welcomed by Wanglat during her maiden visit to Arunachal Pradesh to inaugurate the Borduria Church

Mother Teresa inaugurates the Borduria Catholic Church in the presence of the Chief of Borduria, DC, Tirap and Archbishop Thomas Menamparambil

Mother Teresa discussing the establishment of the Missionaries of Charity in Tirap District with Wanglat

Mother Teresa presenting the Holy Bible to Mrs. Wanglat

Mother Teresa with Wanglat's son Marcus

Wanglat's mother Senphiak at 98 with Archbishop Thomas

Saint Teresa of Calcutta

Archbishop Thomas Menamparampil of Guwahati

Bishop John Thomas, Itanagar

Bishop P K George, Miao

Bishop Robert Kerketta

Fr. C. C. Jose, SDB the first priest to establish the Itanagar Parish Church

Fr. Job the first officially appointed Parish Priest of Arunachal Pradesh. He was stationed at Naharkatiya, Assam 1978-1980. He was the first Catholic Priest to have been officially convicted for violation of Inner-Line pass under 1873 ABFR Act

Col. K. A. A. Raja, the first Lt. Governor of Arunachal Pradesh (the principal architect of persecution of Christians in Arunachal Pradesh)

The first five Councillors of Arunachal Pradesh with Chief Commissioner, Col. K. A. A. Raja (third from the left in a black suit. L-R: Wangpha Lowang, late Tomo Riba, former CM, Raja, P. K. Thungon, former CM who piloted the APFRA 1979, late Sobang Teyang, Councillor who became Minister, late Tadar Tang, Councillor who became Minister. This team passed a resolution forfeiting stipends and other facilities granted to Arunachal scheduled tribes and students for accepting the Christian Faith

Dr Daying Ering, the first Arunachalee Christian to be appointed as Union Parliamentary Secretary and Dy. Minister for Food and Agriculture

Late Bakin Pertin, for MP from Pasighat. He vehemently spoke against the APFRA 1978 in the Parliament. He was an associate member of the Janata Party and resigned to join the Indian National Congress. He was very close to Indira Gandhi. She advised him to take a delegation to Arunachal Pradesh to study the persecution of Christians. The team members included late P. A. Sangma, Speaker of the Lok Sabha, late G. S. Reddy, MP, late Ms. R. Shaiza, MP, Hopingstone Lyngdoh, MP along with Fr. M. C. Thomas, the Bishop of Dibrugarh, late Tadar Teniang, former Minister, L. M. Yanger, General Secretary, ACAC, late Revered C. L. Rima, late Yontam Lego, Reverend Khoda Tana, Baptist Field Secretary, Boa Tado, former MLA and L. Wanglat, former Minister

Late Tomo Riba, former CM, and MP, who opposed the enactment of the Arunachal Pradesh Freedom of Religions Act, 1978 in the state assembly and he along with all PPA members walked out of the House as a mark of protest

Khoda Tana Tara, first Field Secretary of Subansiri Baptist Church Council. He was held and tortured for a week by persecutors

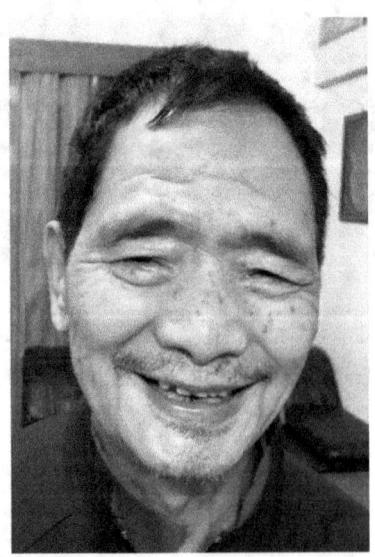

Neelam Taram, former Home Minister. He was captured and beaten up in Ziro

Robin Hibu, IPS. Additional CP, a practicing Christian who is actively serving people in the Northeast of the country through his association with "Helping Hands"

Kimi Aya, IPS, SSP, a dedicated Catholic officer from the Apatani Tribe

Photograph taken in 2019 of bishops and priests participating in their priestly religious rites. They are all non-tribals and none of them are from Arunachal Pradesh

www.ingramcontent.com/pod-product-compliance
Lightning Source LLC
LaVergne TN
LVHW011944060526
838201LV00061B/4205